I0030311

HUMAN RESOURCES AT ITS BEST!

How to manage an HR Department

ROBERTA CAVA

Copyright © 2013 by Roberta Cava

All rights reserved. No part of this work covered by the copyrights hereon may be reproduced or used in any form or by any means - graphic, electronic or mechanical, including photocopying, recording, taping or information storage and retrieval systems - without the prior written permission of the publisher.

Human Resources at its Best!

How to Manage an HR Department

Roberta Cava

Published by Cava Consulting

105 / 3 Township Drive,

Burleigh Heads, 4220, Queensland, Australia

info@dealingwithdifficultpeople.info

Discover other titles by Roberta Cava at
www.dealingwithdifficultpeople.info

National Library of Australia

Cataloguing-in-publication data:

ISBN 978-0-9923402-7-8

BOOKS BY ROBERTA CAVA

Dealing with Difficult People

(21 publishers – in 16 languages)

Dealing with Difficult Situations – at Work and at Home

Dealing with Difficult Spouses and Children

Dealing with Difficult Relatives and In-Laws

Dealing with Domestic Violence and Child Abuse

Dealing with School Bullying

Dealing with Workplace Bullying

What am I going to do with the rest of my life?

Before tying the knot – Questions couples Must ask each other
Before they marry!

How Women can advance in business

Survival Skills for Supervisors and Managers

Human Resources at its Best!

Easy Come – Hard to go – The Art of Hiring, Disciplining and
Firing Employees

Time and Stress – Today's silent killers

Take Command of your Future – Make things Happen

Belly Laughs for All! – Volumes 1 to 4

Wisdom of the World! The happy, sad and wise things in life!

ACKNOWLEDGEMENTS

My gratitude is extended to the companies I have helped set up their Human Resources Departments. I learned as much from them as they did from me.

Special thanks go to the participants of my *'Managing the Human Resources Function'* seminars. They too helped me keep abreast of what was happening in the field of Human Resources in their countries.

DEDICATION

Dedicated to the many government departments that have kept me up-to-date relating to Human Resources matters.

HUMAN RESOURCES AT ITS BEST!

How to Manage an HR Department

Table of Contents

Trouble signs to watch for
What should interviewers guard against?
What can be asked on application forms and interviews?
Questions often asked of women on interviews
Why are applicants rejected?
Transferrable skills

Reference Checks
Important questions to ask
Who should you contact?
The Job Offer
Sample job offer
If the candidate accepts the position
The first day

Performance Appraisals
Planning a performance appraisal interview
Why are Performance Appraisals held?
How to provide the right climate
Levels of Performance
How often are Performance Appraisals completed?
Who should conduct Performance Appraisal interviews?
What information should be on an employee's personnel
    file?

What motivates most employees?
Maslow's Hierarchy of Needs
De-motivating factors
Common ways we see anger expressed at work
The Right of appeal

Qualities of a good trainer
Teaching adults
Characteristics of adult learners
Differences in adult/child learners
Learning process
How to 'lock in' training

One-on-one training
Determining training needs
Testing abilities of employees
Dimensions tested
Manpower planning
Training needs of supervisors
Learning a new skill
Training of others
Retention of information
Training vs. development
Career development
Training procedure
Tangible/intangible behaviour
Setting objectives
Sample objectives
Identifying costs of training
Methods of instruction
Methods I use
Preparing for a seminar/workshop
Group vs. individual activities
Technical vs. life skills
Theoretical vs. practical training
Bridging
Timing of training segments
Use of training aids
Re-enforcement of training
How to keep participants motivated
Instructor's apparel
Presentation skills
Training Agreements

Why managers hate disciplining their staff
Firing probationary employees
Disciplining former peers
Differences between counselling and disciplinary
    interviews
Interview objectives
Interview pointers
Where should interviews be held?
Counselling Interviews – when they are warranted
Difficult counselling interviews

Planning a counselling interview
Conducting a counselling interview
Documentation
Follow-up
Questioning employees
Maintaining improved performance
When no improvement is clear

Chapter 8 – Discipline Problems

Absenteeism
Absenteeism policies
Overlong lunch hour
Coffee break abuses
Smoke Break Abuses
Personality conflicts
Buck-passing employees
Bottleneck employees
Aggressive attitude
Ethnic problems
Personal telephone calls
Mistake-ridden employees
When to interfere in personal employee problems
Employee daydreaming
Disorganised or messy work area
Supply theft
Alcoholic employee
Sexual harassment
What is sexual harassment?
Where does sexual harassment happen?
Who is liable for discrimination and sexual
   harassment?
How does sexual harassment affect others?
Model sexual harassment policy
Workplace bullying
Who are the targets of bullying?
How to deal with workplace bullying
Model bullying, harassment and violence policy

Chapter 9 – Disciplinary Interviews

Preparing yourself psychologically
The disciplinary procedure
Disciplinary interviews

Conducting disciplinary interviews
Documentation
Types of disciplinary action
Termination/dismissal/firing
How to investigate an incident
Exit interviews
Model exit interviews
Purpose of exit interviews

INTRODUCTION

My seminar *'Managing the Human Resources Function'* and ultimately this book evolved because I kept seeing the poor job most companies were doing in managing their Human Resources Departments. Most simply promoted one of their managers to look after that function and expected them to be able to run that department with no training in how to do so. What a mistake! A company's biggest asset is their employees and if they aren't dealt with fairly – the company can't function to its full capacity.

Human Resources includes the following areas:

- Ensure that all employment laws are enforced
- Writing Human Resources Policies and Procedures
- Preparing Employee Handbooks
- Hiring the right employees to fill positions in the company
- Checking references before employee is hired
- Writing Job Descriptions
- Classifying Positions
- Wage and Salary Surveys
- Manpower Planning
- Performance Appraisals
- Managing employee's confidential Personnel Files
- Finding ways to keep employees motivated to do a good job
- Employee relations to deal with employee problems
- Liaising with management, union and employees
- Determining training needs
- Training and development of staff
- Manage training agreements
- Career development
- Conducting counselling interviews

- Conducting Disciplinary interviews

- Writing written warnings

- When necessary, firing / terminating employees

- Laying off or making positions redundant when required

- Dealing with personality conflicts between supervisors, unions and employees

Many companies do not have proper job descriptions. They expect a simple paragraph to describe what their employees do to complete their tasks. Then they have the audacity to conduct performance appraisals when neither the supervisor nor the employee has anything in writing about what they are evaluating. Many performance appraisals evaluate subjective, rather than objective issues. No wonder there's chaos in some companies.

Other Human Resources Managers have had no formal training in how to counsel employees, yet they are responsible for the Employee Relations function of their company. They are the ones that should be mediating during disputes between staff and management. They are the liaison between unions and management.

If they don't take enough time when hiring employees, they'll be setting themselves up for a period of misery. If they don't know how to find and/or provide the necessary training employees need to do their jobs effectively – the tasks won't be completed properly. If they ask discriminatory questions on the interview and they don't hire the candidate – that candidate can charge the company with discrimination. And if the employee's behaviour or productivity becomes a problem – do they have the knowledge to discipline and/or fire that employee. In many cases they don't, so companies end up in court being charged with wrongful dismissal.

The contents of this book are not to be construed as being professional advice. Readers must always check their Federal and State laws to ensure that they are acting according to their laws. Any decision made by the reader as a result of reading this book, is the sole responsibility of the reader.

CHAPTER ONE

HIRING THE RIGHT EMPLOYEES

When hiring employees, problems can occur if:

- The right questions aren't asked on the interview;
- The interviewers aren't knowledgeable enough to hire competent personnel; and
- References aren't checked properly.

Companies may end up with a bad employee who, instead of helping their company with production, cause more work in the long run. Have you hired someone and found that:

a) They lied on the interview about how long they worked for a company?

b) They told you they had more experience than they actually had?

c) They weren't able to handle the duties of the position after considerable in-house or professional training?

d) Their supervisor was on a different wave-length than the new employee and found it difficult to get him/her to do things the way s/he wanted them done?

e) The company required a self-starter and the employee required very detailed instructions to complete any job?

f) The person was hired to work on the front lines dealing directly with clients but you've found that they don't have the people-skills required for them to do a good job?

g) The person whines and complains about everything which eventually rubs off on their co-workers and causes low morale in their department?

h) Your company has installed a new computer system, but the new employee is unwilling or unable to pick up the new technology?

i) They didn't fit in with the existing staff?

j) Their work ethic left much to be desired?

k) The person procrastinates or is a perfectionist so that project deadlines aren't met?

l) The employee is a know-it-all, doesn't follow directions, does things his/her own way and bucks the system?

m) The person looked very presentable on the interview, but their day-to-day appearance leaves much to be desired even after several requests from his/her supervisor?

I'm sure you've run into the above kinds of employees in your daily work situation. Proper interviewing, screening and reference checking of the above employees would have eliminated most of those problems.

Unfortunately it seems the more lazy and crafty the employee, the harder they seem to get rid of. So doing things right (before they're hired) is crucial. Does this take a lot of training? No, it doesn't but it will certainly help to know how to get the information you require to choose the best candidate for the position. Some interviewers felt as if they were being interviewed by the candidate rather than the other way around, but didn't know how to get the interview back on track.

Shortage of Good Employees

In addition to the pending shortage of workers, many jobs will require skills that available workers simply don't have. In tomorrow's high-tech workplaces, simple entry-level jobs will be almost nonexistent. The inroads of microprocessors, electronic components and the ability to read and understand technical manuals will keep many from doing what used to be simple tasks.

Where immigrant workers in the past could be shown how to use a machine and do their job, they're now required to read instructions, gauges, printouts and graphs so require a good command of English.

Unfortunately, many applicants for clerical positions aren't able to pass even simple reading and math tests. While the calibre of applicants for entry-level positions is declining, the level of skills required for the same jobs is rising, creating an employee vacuum that companies are scrambling to fill. In the past, many employers saved their training dollars for their supervisory or management staff, but they're finding it necessary to spend almost as much getting their entry-level people up to the standards they require for them to do a good job.

Other firms find that those in entry-level positions are bored and give poor performance. To eliminate this, they've initiated job rotation to keep the employees interested. Training is the answer to many of the foregoing problems. Companies will be forced to spend more money to fill the gap between job requirements and the employee's skills and abilities. Many corporations will pay more attention to Human Resources because of this.

Part-time Employees

Companies have been hiring clerical, drafting and other people by the hour for decades. With an increasing shortage of qualified people, companies will take advantage of others they may not have considered hiring as part-time help in the past. Although rates may be comparable to full-time salaries, the company won't have to pay bonuses, benefits or payroll taxes.

Those who know how to use word-processors, but don't wish to work in an office setting, could have the option of working out of their homes. Their companies will provide a computer and the employee will contact the office once or twice a week, take home the work and deliver the finished product the next time they visit the office. The use of FAX machines and e-mail even make that unnecessary.

Temporary executives can be hired on a contract basis to fill recurring as well as one-time employment needs. For example, during a company merger, a temporary executive versed in these matters, will be hired to oversee the changeover. Another company could hire a computer expert to look after the installation of a highly sophisticated computer and in the training of staff required to run it.

A company may decide to cut their in-house training staff down to one person who determines training needs. After doing so s/he will hire outside trainers to fill identified needs or send employees to courses provided by learning institutes.

A part-time executive might be hired to work along with first-time entrepreneurs to help them during their critical start-up stage. Small businesses will hire a Human Resources expert on a part-time basis to help them with hiring initial staff, setting up personnel files, writing job descriptions, classifying jobs, setting salary ranges, instructing on how to conduct a performance appraisal, helping with determining training needs, advising on disciplinary matters and conducting exit interviews.

It's certainly an option to consider part-time executives before taking on the expense of hiring a full-time employee. So your first step is to hire the right employee for the right job.

Mandate of Employers

The first aim of most companies is to make a profit. They need to offer a work environment in which employees want and are able to do the things that are required for the company or organisation to be successful.

Mandate of Supervisors/Managers

Supervisors and managers need to give their employees all the tools they need to complete their tasks properly. This means providing on-the-job or formal training to fill the gap between the employee's skills and the requirements of the job. It means that they are available and willing to help employees with support and advice. Supervisors need to keep in mind that a bad employee reflects directly upon *them*. Not only does the employee look bad but so does his/her supervisor – so the supervisor must ensure that the employee is doing his/her job effectively.

Mandate of Employees

Employees' mandate is much simpler. Their mandate is simply to make their bosses look good! Employees need to understand what is expected of them and have an earnest desire to want to improve their behaviour and performance to meet identified standards of performance.

What will your company offer the employee for his/her services?

In addition to salaries, there are many perks that a company can offer a candidate to get the best person for the job. Some of these perks are:

- Relocation allowance;
- Shorter probationary period;
- Placed on company benefit plans immediately;
- Guaranteed paid training programs;
- Longer vacations;
- Corner office with windows;

- Rug on floor, upscale furniture, plants and decorating;
- Company car;
- Company expense account;
- Prestigious title;
- Stock options;
- Company savings plans;
- Interest-free loans;
- Health club membership;
- Own support staff;
- Private bathroom;
- Own boardroom;
- Guaranteed salary increases; and/or
- Free tax expert to help with income tax returns.

Employment Interview Objectives

Before you prepare for an interview, it's important to focus your attention on what you're trying to achieve at the employment interview. This is:

- To determine candidates' qualifications compared to the requirements of a particular position;
- To learn what a candidate has to offer your company for future vacancies;
- To give the candidate the opportunity of learning about your company and the position.

These objectives are met by:

a) Gathering information;
b). Pinpointing unique characteristics such as:

1. Ambition;
2. Ability;
3. Energy level;
4. Interpersonal skills;
5. Loyalty towards their profession and former companies;
6. Knowledge of themselves;
7. Motivational factors;
8. Leadership capacity;
9. Judgement and foresight;
10. Decisiveness;

11. Persistence;
12. Emotional stability;
13. Personal grooming;
14. Poise;
15. Education and training.

c). Level of knowledge (compared to education);
d). Assess compatibility with proposed work group.

The employment interview can be the most valuable step in the entire process of employee selection. It can tell you more of what you need to know about a candidate than any of the other selection tools. Therefore, it's crucial that interview time is spent effectively. Proper preparation before the interview is essential.

How candidates will apply for vacancies:

There are five ways that candidates will likely apply for vacancies:

a) Person fills in your company application form. Most companies suggest that applicants send in a resume in addition to filling out their application form.

b) A Chronological resume which gives the candidate's experience in a chronological manner, with their last position listed first on their resume. These include such headings as:

- Education (including seminars they may have attended);
- Work experience (both part- and full-time);
- Membership and Activities;
- References.

c) A Functional resume which identifies the unique talents and abilities of the candidate (often referred to as transferrable skills.) These include such headings as:

- Education (including seminars they may have attended);
- Work experience (both part- and full-time). Headings under this category would include:
  o Working with data;
  o Dealing with People;
  o Management experience;

- o Scheduling;
- o Accounting knowledge;
- o Computer knowledge;
- o Specific projects, etc.
- Dates of employment (with list of companies they worked for and positions held; specific duties aren't listed);
- Membership and Activities;
- References.

d) Combination Resume. As you'd expect – it's a combination of the Chronological and Functional resumes. Not only does it identify the person's transferrable skills, but also identifies the companies where those skills were gained. Instead of elaborate information about what the person did for the companies, just the company, position and dates of employment are identified after the transferrable skills are given.

e) The person may present a Portfolio showing examples of their past work. This is normally accompanied by a resume of some sort.

Let's assume you've gone through the screening process and you've set up interviews to fill the position. Where do you start?

Hiring that New Employee

There are several stages one must go through before hiring a new employee:

Step One

Position is vacated or new position established.

Step Two

The job description is checked to see whether it is up-to-date and accurate. This is one of the most crucial steps and one that most people neglect. If there isn't a job description available, prepare one (see Chapter 4 to learn how to do this).

Step Three

Using the information gleaned from the position's up-to-date job description, prepare a candidate specification sheet to identify the necessary education and experience requirements. (Try not to be too rigid). Ask yourself, *'Do we really need this level of education and/or experience?'* Determine equivalencies you will consider in candidates. Much of this information will be found on the position description.

Step Four

The position is advertised. Now that you're aware of what kind of person you're looking for, you'll have to write an advertisement to attract suitable candidates. This could be through company bulletins, newspaper, on-line or other media. A well-written advertisement lets the candidates know exactly what qualifications you'll be requiring. It's a good idea to include a deadline for applications and if you're in a hurry, ask the candidates to send their information via e-mail, but they may do so via facsimile or regular mail. Be careful when writing advertisements that you do not break the anti-discrimination laws relating to gender, age, cultural backgrounds etc. (See Chapter 2 for Anti-Discrimination Act, 1991.)

Step Five

Resumes/applications are screened against the candidate specifications. If candidates require three years' directly related experience (be reasonable when requesting this). Be sure to determine what directly related experience is. If several of the candidates only have only one or two years' experience - eliminate them. Make a short list of the best candidates that fit the education and experience requirements.

Step Six

All rejected candidates should receive a 'Dear John' or 'Dear Jane' letter as soon as you make that decision. This leaves them free to pursue other ventures. Many companies don't do this, which is extremely discourteous to prospective employees.

The candidates deserve to know as soon as possible, whether they're going to be asked for an interview or are rejected at the onset. If possible tell them where they fell short in their experience or education (or whatever else was lacking. You might even suggest a different kind of work as being more suitable for them).

Step Seven

Those that are not screened out are invited for an interview. Make sure you leave sufficient time between interviews so you can carefully examine the candidate's qualifications against each other.

Step Eight

Before your first interview, prepare a list of the personal qualities you will be looking for in the candidates you interview. (See Chapter 2 about Evaluating Candidates.)

Step Nine

Conduct the actual interviews.

How long should interviews last?

As long as it takes to ensure you have evaluated the candidate fairly and have obtained all the information you need to make your hiring decision. Many companies cheat the candidate (and themselves) by not allowing enough time to really get to know the candidate. Clerical positions warrant at least thirty minutes. Higher, more complex positions should be longer - some take several hours, a tour of your facilities, seeing where they would be working, etc. Top management candidates often come back several times with as many as five or six interviews comprising one to two hours spent with company representatives. So be prepared to take as long as it requires to hire the right person.

If you've ever been interviewed yourself, you can relate to the first five or ten minutes of an interview. Were you acting like the 'real you?' Or were you nervous, fidgety, aloof, shy, talked too much, etc? Were you more like your real self later on in the interview? I'm sure you'll agree that the candidates you're hiring deserve this same courtesy. Also recognise that if you reject the person in the first four or five minutes of the interview (as many hiring personnel do) your body language and tone of voice will clue them in that you've done so. The 'break the ice' stage will never be crossed, because they'll know at the onset that you're not going to listen to what they have to say.

Stop yourself if you make snap judgments on candidates. Be fair and give them the opportunity of presenting themselves in a better light. This won't occur if you've pre-judged them in the first few minutes before candidates have a chance to really be themselves and present their qualifications fairly.

Recognise that if you are a very people-oriented person and are hiring an engineer or accountant who are more comfortable working alone, you might not consider them good candidates because they are not clones of yourself. So be fully aware of what kind of personality would suit each position.

Step Ten

After the interview, make notes on your findings about the candidate, evaluate them against the requirements of the position, against other candidates for personal qualities and come up with one or two top candidates. Do this as soon as your interview is over (not at the end of several interviews, otherwise you will mix up your reactions to different candidates). Before the next interview, be sure to go over the next candidate's resume so you're fully prepared to re-channel your full attention to their interview.

Step Eleven

Check references of your top two candidates then choose the best one to fill the vacancy. (See Chapter 3 for more details on reference checking.)

Step Twelve

A verbal job offer is extended. If your verbal offer is accepted, a written job offer is mailed or delivered to the successful candidate. (See Chapter 3 for information on how to accomplish this).

Step Thirteen

The employee starts his or her new job.

Start your new employee properly. Formal orientation programs are a good first step toward integrating new employees into your staff. That orientation will explain the rules, regulations, policies and procedures of your company and give them an Employee Handbook (see Chapter 4) that includes written rules of your company along with general policies and procedures.

Because new employees usually learn the 'real' ropes from their peers, introduce him/her to the rest of the staff, then appoint an 'old timer' (usually long-term employee) or friendly workmate who 'adopts' the newcomer. This person acts as their guide. Many new employees have questions they're afraid may sound stupid to their supervisor. They feel more at ease asking a workmate than asking their boss. The helper shows the new employee where the washroom is, when and where to go for coffee and lunch breaks and make them feel welcome with other workmates and lets them in on office politics. This takes the edge off the situation for the new employee in a way that the supervisor could not. It also introduces them to their new peer group. The supervisor's role is to set the atmosphere, then back off to let it work.

We all know how difficult it is the first two weeks on a new job. Set up an appointment with them two weeks after they begin work so you can keep in touch with the new employee to see if there are any problems.

Step Fourteen

Make sure that training is extended to fill any gaps between the candidate's qualifications and the requirements of the job.

Stages of employment interviews

Stage 1: 'Breaking the Ice'

This is usually a simple exchange between people who've just met. Offer a handshake when meeting the candidate and introduce him/her to the members of the panel (if it is a panel interview).

This is the part of the interview where you'll probably indulge in a little 'small talk.' Although this chatter may seem quite removed from the evaluation of the candidate's credentials, it gives the candidate a chance to 'get his/her breath.' It also gives candidates an opportunity to get a feeling about their interviewer(s). You might discuss something of interest from their resume, such as their being a coach of a little-league hockey team. You might be interested in this, so you could discuss this for a moment or two.

When you feel the candidate is more at ease (watch for physical signs, such as sitting back in their chair) let them know what you'll be doing during the interview. This eliminates the possibility of the candidate trying to control the interview sequence. You want to know what they have to offer your company, before they learn what you're specifically looking for. If they know ahead of time, they may feed you the information they think you're looking for.

To inform the candidate of the sequencing of the interview you may say, *'First we'd like to go over your resume with you and ask some questions regarding your experience. Next we'll discuss the responsibilities of the position. There will be time at the end of the interview for any questions you may have. If you don't understand any question, please ask. We want this to be an information-sharing session rather than us asking you questions.'*

Stage 2: 'Information Giving'

This stage of the interview focuses on the candidate's background and general qualifications. This is where the interviewers try to determine how well the candidate's qualifications match up with the requirements of the position. ***Remember to keep all questions job-related.***

Stage 3: 'Selling'

This is the stage where you describe the duties of the position and candidates have the opportunity of selling themselves. Examples of questions to ask:

'How does your education prepare you for this position?'

'What work experience do you have that makes you suitable for this position?'

'What are your strengths/weaknesses?

Stage 4: 'Tying it all together'

The fourth and final stage of the interview consists of the closing comments that tie the interview together. This is where you encourage candidates to ask questions about issues not covered earlier in the interview. Candidates may or may not have written questions. The fact that they came prepared for this area of the interview should give them 'Brownie Points.' Candidates would ask such questions as:

'What are my chances of promotion in your area?'

'What kind of group will I be working with?'

'How many people are in this department?'

'How long would my probationary period be?'

'What kind of computer will I be working with?'

'Is there much travel with this job?'

Be ready with answers or tell them you'll get back to them later, if they ask a question you can't answer.

CHAPTER TWO

EMPLOYMENT INTERVIEW TIPS

In Chapter 1 we discussed the overall steps you would take to conduct an effective employment interview. Here are the additional pieces of information that can enhance the flow of the interview process.

One of the first steps in the interview process is coming up with an accurate up-to-date job description.

Job Descriptions

Every position (not just groups of positions) should have accurate, up-too-date job descriptions. Many companies update their job descriptions when they conduct their annual performance appraisals. These companies fully understand that if the employee doesn't know what they're supposed to do (and their supervisor doesn't know either) - how can supervisors possibly evaluate how well their employees are performing their tasks?

Job descriptions should include all the information you'd want, if you were filling the position. *Remember, that Job Descriptions describe the position - not the person filling it.*

All Job Descriptions must have:

1. A general paragraph describing the position.
2. KPIs (Key Performance Indicators). These are the main functions of the job.
3. List of tasks that are necessary to meet the KPIs.
4. Standards of performance for each task under the KPI.

Standards of performance:

Job descriptions and performance appraisals should both have detailed standards of performance to clarify what is expected of employees. A Standard of Performance is a yardstick against which performance in a particular part of a job is measured. It's usually a series of brief statements of the quality and quantity expected within specific time frames and identifies the costs (in time and/or money).

For example:

Task: Hire three sales personnel

Standard of performance:

Hire three sales personnel who have a minimum of three years' directly related experience by May 1, 20___, at a salary range of $30,000 to $35,000 per annum.

Quality: 3 years' directly related experience. (You'd have to establish what 'directly related experience' really means).

Quantity: 3 sales personnel

Time: By May 1, 20 __.

Cost: Salary range of $30,000 to 35,000 per annum.

When setting Standards of Performance, consider:

- The performance of other people in similar situations. (Watch you don't choose a high or low achiever's performance as 'average!');
- Engineered or prevailing standards;
- Employees' past performance on the job as shown from their previous performance appraisals;
- What managers and employees negotiate as reasonable.

Advantages of setting standards of performance:

A worker, who knows his or her job has certain specific standards, is always aware of how s/he is doing. Employees can rate their own job effectiveness and start improvement in unsatisfactory areas without waiting for appraisals from their managers.

Standards of Performance enable the manager to evaluate his or her whole department realistically. Managers can spot areas where individual employees need improvement, take steps to improve the whole group and recognise superior performance.

Standards make it possible to base performance rating on something more objective than personality traits and surface impressions (i.e. judgement, initiative, interpersonal skills and attitude). They keep the personalities out of it and deal only with the actual output of the employee.

Some sample headings on Job Descriptions are:

Title of Position:
Position #:
Location:
Hours of work:
Department, branch or unit:
Reports to:
Job Summary: (in paragraph form - just giving a brief description of the position).
Duties and Responsibilities: (showing percentage of time spent on each duty or weighting in importance.)

- Start with Key Performance Indicators (KPIs). These are the major functions of the job. For instance:
  (KPI) Responsible for all company training.
- Under each KPI, list all the tasks that must be performed to achieve the KPI.
  For instance: (Task)
  Ensure that all supervisors and managers receive our approved 3-day supervisory training course by June 1st, 20____ for a yearly cost of less than $120,000.
- Under each task, list the standards of performance relating to that task:
  For example: (Standard of Performance)
  Quality: Approved 3-day supervisory training course.
  Quantity: All supervisors and managers.
  Time: June 1st, 20____.
  Cost: Less than $120,000.

Work Complexity: Such as choice of action, consequences of error, difficulty or work pressures, contacts, confidentiality).
Supervision received: (level, how much independent action).
Whom position supervises: (Titles of positions direct or indirect supervision. Do they assign work? Review work? Conduct performance appraisals? Discipline subordinates?)
Working conditions: (be specific about adverse conditions).
Equipment used: (be specific).
Qualifications required: such as formal education, experience, specific skills, licenses or certificates.
Physical requirements: (i.e. employee must be able to handle packages weighing up to 10 kg).
Probationary period:
Promotional opportunities:

No more than 10% of their duties should be identified as: 'Other Duties as Assigned.'

If the employee performs the duty every day, every week or once every year - it should be on his or her position description.

Why is probationary period included on a position description? While an employee's on probation, there's far less paperwork if you wish to fire them because of inadequate performance. The employee would probably want to know how long the probationary period is, because many companies don't put employees on full company benefits until their probationary period is over.

How long should a probationary period be? I recommend three months. Most companies have anywhere from three months to one year. If employees have to wait a full year to receive company benefits (which can be 30 to 50 per cent of their base salary) they'd miss a lot of extra money. It's also a long time to be on 'tender-hooks' wondering if they're going to be accepted as a full-time employee. Some union agreements stipulate set probationary periods.

Promotional opportunities need to be listed as well. If candidates are 'fast-trackers' you'll lose them if they're placed in a dead-ended position with little chance of promotion. On the other hand, many people are not 'fast-trackers' and would be content staying in one position for a long time.

Sample Job Description

[Company Logo]

Position Description

Position Title
Salary Range
Department/Location
Number of Reports: Direct? Indirect?
Reports to: (title)
Working Conditions:
[Work setting, stresses of the job, deadline-prone activities, requirement to deal with difficult clients, colleagues, pressures

from many departments, quotas to meet, inside, outside, special conditions etc.]

Work Complexity:
[Such as choice of action, consequences of error, work pressures, contacts, confidentiality]

Position Summary: [In paragraph form – just giving a brief description of the position]

List Key Performance Indicators/Objectives:
1. Identify the Key Performance Indicator. [i.e.: Hire competent staff].
2. List the tasks that will be performed to reach the Key Performance Indicator.
3. Give a weight to the importance of each task. (Total for *all* tasks performed on Job Description must not be more than 100%.)
4. Make sure each task has Standards of Performance i.e.: When setting standards of performance, keep in mind how you will measure whether the task has been completed properly. This usually includes:
   Quality: Several years' directly related experience in the retail business;
   Quantity: 3 sales representatives;
   Time: By May 1, 20___
   Cost: Salary range of $45,000 - $50,000 per annum;

Key Performance Indicator/Objective

(Hire 3 sales representatives)
Weight of each task: [how important is this responsibility compared to other responsibilities]
Tasks:
Standards of Performance

Key Performance Indicator/Objective
(Hire 2 Classification Clerk 1 staff)
Weight of each task: [how important is this responsibility compared to other responsibilities]
Tasks:
Standards of Performance
[Add other tasks to the list and go to the next items]
Decision-making authority:
Key Customers: Internal? External?
Equipment Used:

Probationary Period:
Promotional Opportunities: [What is the career path for this position?]
Medical Requirements of Position: [Be careful with this one – it must be a true requirement]
Key Competencies:

- Experience/Qualifications:
- Knowledge:
- Skills:
- Attributes/Behaviours:

Job descriptions are used to determine which classification and salary range the position is in as it relates to others in the company. This is becoming increasingly more important as pay equity becomes law. There are three areas of law that are becoming more important in business. So you will understand the differences between the three equity issues:

Pay equity:

Is a system that determines the value of the position as it compares to that of others in the company. It compares 'apples against oranges' or 'accountants, engineers, production people, caretakers, personal assistants and managers' against the value of all other employees in the company. Australia has yet to implement these laws.

Pay equity uses job descriptions to see if the positions have been evaluated properly and given equitable salary ranges to meet the requirements of the position. It examines such things as working conditions, knowledge, experience, education etc. and gives points for each of these. This way companies can compare all positions in their company. All companies are encouraged to be ready for these changes. Under pay equity laws, companies are required to have an evaluation system that's used to evaluate even the highest position in the company against the value of the lowest and determine salary ranges to suit the work performed.

To make pay equity work, all job descriptions will require that all tasks are described clearly (i.e. detailed, quantitative and measurable). In order to accomplish this, standards of performance will be required to explain how each task is performed.

Equal Pay for work of equal value:

This compares cooks vs. chefs; cleaning ladies vs. janitors for instance and ensures that if men and women are doing essentially the same kind of task – regardless of the title – they must be paid the same.

Employment Equity:

This relates to anti-discrimination and equal opportunity laws that protect minorities from discrimination.

Classification of Positions

The first step in evaluating a position is the preparation of an accurate up-to-date job description which clearly states the responsibility, authority and qualifications required to fill the position. Next the position is graded against an established rating which determines the value of each factor as it relates to the needs of the position. Points are allotted to the above grades and the total point score of the position determines the salary range for the position. This way, accountants can be compared with engineers, secretaries with custodians.

There are many forms of classification systems. The most popular in North America are the Hay and Kellogg systems. These are systems where every position in a company can be compared against a factor system that ensures fair payment for work performed (pay equity).

These systems evaluate (with points) the comparative worth of every position. Each factor determines the level required for each position to be effectively filled by an employee. It does not take into account gender, race or colour, just the requirements of the position. These factors evaluate such things as:

Knowledge and Ability:

1. Complexity - Judgement
2. Education
3. Experience (related)
4. Initiative (Independent action)

Responsibilities:

1. Errors (consequences of)
2. Contacts (level)
3. Supervision - (responsibility level)
4. Supervision - Scope (how many)

Physical Conditions:

1. Physical Demands
2. Working Conditions

When those factors are determined and the value to the company of the contribution made by the employee in the position is determined, a salary range is chosen for the position.

To this date, not much has changed. In many companies you'll find that only a small segment of employees (the middle group) has been evaluated fairly by their company's evaluation system. If lower and upper level positions are examined, it's often found that incorrect salary ranges have been allotted. In most cases, lower-level employees are underpaid - and upper-level staff were grossly overpaid!

If these old job-classification systems had been implemented correctly, women working in personal assistant and clerical positions would have been paid as much as technicians, because of their specialised knowledge and skills. Many support positions require the same length of training and have similar working conditions as technologists' jobs. However, this is not reflected in the salary structures for the two types of jobs.

Worldwide, much effort has been put into dealing with gender bias in job evaluation systems. Many countries have found that legislative rulings were necessary to eliminate gender bias from the job evaluation process. Before this was implemented many women found:

- Gender-stereotyping which could result in the under-evaluation of female-held positions.
- Many evaluations of female-held positions underestimated the importance of the skills and qualities required.

However, many businesses believe that legislation to bring in equal pay for work of equal value - to equalise the salary structures for *different* but equally important jobs - will cripple their companies will destroy them. In a way, you can't blame them for opposing such legislation. They believe they cannot afford to implement this policy in a tight economy and heaven forbid - they may have to take a pay cut themselves!

Business owners contend they can't afford to make these essential changes, but an imaginative approach to the problem would enable them to do so. Until pay equity is achieved, those who've been overpaid (according to fair and realistic job-evaluation criteria) would have their salaries frozen and those whose positions have been undervalued, would be paid a regular salary increase plus a portion of the increase that would normally have gone to the 'frozen' employee. Companies would not lose money under such a scheme, but we can see why there's such resistance to pay equity by the upper level decision-makers in industry. They're the ones who would be having their salaries frozen!

How to conduct a wage and salary survey:

You may want to conduct these from time to time to determine whether your company's salaries are comparable and equitable to others in your industry. These are accomplished by:

- Watching newspaper advertisements;
- Comparing through organisations/associations such as (engineering, accounting, etc.);
- Checking with universities, colleges, re surveys they might have completed;
- Comparing to your competition's wages;
- Checking State and Federal governments for their listing of normal salaries.

Knowing your employees better:

A company's most valuable asset is its people. Unless you know your staff well, you're probably not going to take advantage of their unique talents and abilities. Supervisors can get to know their staff much better by going over their resume or application form with them. Even if their staff have worked for them for three years, there are likely things they've done in the past that the supervisor may not aware of. They'd find this information on the employee's application form and/or resume.

After discussing his/her history, they would go over the position description with them. They might determine the following with their employee's assistance:

a) Which tasks are the most important (what you think are most important may not be the same as those the employee chooses!)

b) How much time do you spend on each task? Work out in percentages and put next to the task.

c) Which duties would you classify as routine duties? Which are periodic duties (once a week, a month etc.) or special projects?

d) Which tasks do you enjoy the most and why? Ask this because you'll know who's likely to be the best qualified to handle a new project. The likelihood of a good job being done is higher if the employee enjoys the tasks they're doing.

e) Which tasks do you dislike the most and why? You will probably have to watch these employees more closely because you'll know they dislike this kind of task. You may consider delegating tasks of this nature to someone else that doesn't have this particular dislike.

f) Which tasks do you feel should be handled by someone else? It's possible that the employee is doing step two of a process, while another does step one and three. They may feel (and they could be right) that it would be better if one person handled all three steps.

g) Which tasks do you feel should be assigned to you, but aren't? It's possible they are the ones doing step one and three and also feel that they should be doing step two as well.

h) Is there anything you can do to help them complete their tasks more efficiently?

They may find some unexpected information turns up when they discuss the above questions. In the end, they'll have a job description that's accurate and an employee who knows what s/he's expected to do.

Writing Advertisements

Be extremely careful that you don't break any anti-discrimination laws. When hiring new employees keep in mind the laws that go along with this practice. The following information quotes from the wording used by the Queensland Australia government literature. If you live in another State or country, make yourself aware of your State/Provincial laws, as well as Federal government Anti-discrimination laws and those of the Human Rights and equal Opportunity Commission.

What are some of the issues covered by the Australian Anti-Discrimination Act, 1991?

These acts were enacted to promote fair treatment and equality of opportunity by making unfair discrimination against the law. It gives all of us the right to be treated fairly and to take action if unlawful discrimination occurs. It also places responsibilities on all of us to ensure that unlawful discrimination is minimised or prevented.

It is generally inappropriate and against the law for employers to ask questions on application forms or on interviews and The Act prohibits discrimination on the basis of:

- Sex (whether they are female or male);
- Marital or Parental Status (whether they are married, single, widowed, divorced, separated or living with someone as if they were married {de facto} and whether they have children or not);
- Pregnancy and Breast-feeding;
- Age (whether they are young or old);
- Race;
- Impairment (whether they have or have had a physical, intellectual, psychiatric or mental disability, injury or illness, including whether they are HIV+ or use a guide dog, wheelchair or some other remedial device);
- Religion (whether they have particular religious or spiritual beliefs);
- Political belief or activity;
- Trade union activity;
- Lawful sexual activity (whether they are gay lesbian, heterosexual or bisexual);
- Association with or relation to, a person who has any of the above attributes.

This Act also protects against sexual harassment and prohibits victimisation that happens when someone who has been complained about, threatens or harasses others involved in the complaint. This is a serious matter and strong penalties can be imposed for victimisation.

For most jobs, applicants should not be required to do a medical test before they are employed. If pre-employment medicals are used, they should focus on the specific health risks associated with the job, rather than being a general medical. For example, if the job involves working in a dusty condition, the employer may ask if the applicant has any respiratory illnesses. If there is heavy lifting, they may ask for a medical to prove that they are capable of this requirement.

Applicants should not be required to submit a photo with their application for employment.

Individuals are protected against discrimination when they:

- Apply for a job or try to get into a course;
- Work - whether it is full-time, part-time, casual, temporary or voluntary;
- Attend schools, colleges, universities or other educational institutions;
- Buy things in shops hotels, cafes, restaurants, cinemas, etc.;
- Seek or use services from legal, medical and other professionals, businesses and trades persons;
- Rent a house, flat or apartment, hotel or motel room, caravan, office or shop;
- Purchase land or property;
- Apply for credit or a loan;
- Seek or use the services of state or local governments;
- Join, visit or use the services of a club or similar organisation;
- Deal with banks, superannuation or insurance companies.

Resume acknowledgement letter

When you receive an application or resume – confirm with the sender that you have received it. This is often done over the internet. Here's a sample letter that you could send:

(All applicants who apply to positions with company will receive a variation of the following).

[Company Logo]

[Date]
[Name]
[Address]

Dear [Name]

Thank you for taking the time to apply for the position of [Position] and forwarding your resume. We had many very qualified candidates apply and will require approximately two weeks to read all the responses. Those applicants with the closest fit to the job requirements will be contacted for an interview. All those who miss out this time will be kept on file for future reference.

All applicants will be contacted by phone, mail or email one week after the first short list is made.

We wish you success in finding a position that utilises your qualifications.

Sincerely,
[Name]
[Title]

Unsuitable Candidate's letter

Those candidates that are not going to be invited to an interview because they do not fit your candidate specifications should receive a letter as soon as you make that decision. Don't leave them hanging.

[Company Logo]

[Date]
[Name]
[Address]

Dear [Name]

Thank you for taking the time to apply for the position of [Position]. We had many very qualified candidates apply and are in the process of setting up interviews for the candidates we have short-listed.

At this time we do not intend to pursue your application further, but will keep it on file for three months. If a suitable position becomes vacant, we will contact you.

We wish you success in finding a position that utilises your qualifications.

Sincerely,
[Name]
[Title]

Evaluating candidates:

Step Eight in Chapter 1 mentions how you can evaluate the candidate's compatibility to the position. You may find that some are not applicable to the needs of the position. Choose the ones you think important and award points to each one making sure the total adds up to 100%. Then you'll be able to be much more objective in choosing the best candidate. The one with the highest points gets the job! It keeps you on track.

This chart should be used immediately after each interview so you remember each candidate's qualities:

1. Appearance:

a) Very untidy, poor taste in dress;
b) Somewhat careless about personal appearance;
c) Satisfactory personal appearance;
d) Good taste in dress, very neat.

2. Friendliness:

a) Appears very distant and aloof;
b) Approachable, fairly friendly;
c) Warm, friendly, sociable;
d) Very sociable and outgoing;
e) Extremely friendly and sociable.

3. Poise/Stability:

a) Ill at ease, 'jumpy' and appears nervous;
b) Somewhat tense, is easily irritated;
c) As poised as the average applicant;

d) Sure of self, appears to like crisis more than average person;
e) Extremely well composed, apparently thrives under pressure.

4. Personality:

a) Unsatisfactory for the job;
b) Questionable for this job;
c) Satisfactory for this job;
d) Very desirable for this job;
e) Outstanding for this job.

5. Conversational Ability:

a) Talks very little - expresses self poorly;
b) Tries to express self, but does fair job at best;
c) Average fluency and expression;
d) Talks well and 'to the point;'
e) Excellent expression, extremely forceful.

6. Alertness:

a) Slow to 'catch on;'
b) Rather slow, requires more than average explanation;
c) Grasps ideas with average ability;
d) Quick to understand, perceives well;
e) Exceptionally keen and alert.

7. Information about general work field:

a) Poor knowledge of field;
b) Fair knowledge of field;
c) Informed as the average applicant;
d) Knows more than average applicant;
e) Excellent background and experience.

8. Experience:

a) No relationship between applicant's background and job
   requirements;
b) Fair relationship between applicant's background and job
   requirements;
c) Average amount of meaningful background and experience;
d) Background very good, considerable experience;
e) Excellent background and experience.
f) Overqualified for position

9. Drive:

a) Has poorly defined goals and appears to act without purpose;
b) Appears to set goals too low and to put forth little effort to achieve these;
c) Appears to have average goals - puts forth average effort to reach these;
d) Appears to strive hard, has high desire to achieve;
e) Appears to set high goals and to strive incessantly to achieve them.

10. Overall:

a) Definitely unsatisfactory;
b) Substandard;
c) Average;
d) Definitely above average;
e) Outstanding.

To explain this information in more detail: Let's say you're interviewing for a sales position. You'll probably be looking for specific qualities. These could be appearance, friendliness, knowledge and verbal fluency. Give these scores or values (as long as the total adds up to 100 points). You might give appearance a total of 15 points, using the following criteria. For instance:

a) Very untidy, poor taste in dress: 0
b) Somewhat careless about personal appearance: 0
c) Satisfactory personal appearance: 7
d) Good taste in dress, very neat: 15

Friendliness might have a total of 20 points, using the following criteria:

a) Appears very distant and aloof: 0
b) Approachable, fairly friendly: 5
c) Warm, friendly, sociable: 10
d) Very sociable and outgoing: 15
e) Extremely friendly and sociable: 20

This will assist you in choosing between two very close candidates. It also makes it easier for panel interviewers because it gives objective (not subjective) evaluations. Make sure you leave enough time between interviews to complete this evaluation form. You may have to negotiate with other panel members due to conflicts of evaluation points. Panel members would have to explain why they gave scores higher or lower than the rest of the panel. And you would have to do the same.

Preparing for the employment interview:

There are several things to do so your interviews run efficiently and allow you to obtain the information you require to choose the best person for the position:

1. Write down questions you wish to ask *all* candidates. Write down each candidate's answer to the questions. This is essential, if you hire the individual and find that s/he lied on the interview. For example, you may have asked the candidate if s/he is free to travel two or three days a month and s/he answered that it would be *'No problem.'*

    Later when you told him/her s/he would have to attend a meeting in another city, s/he replied, *'Oh, I couldn't do that - who would look after my children?'* S/he lied on the interview and your interview notes will prove this. This would be grounds for dismissal.

    Another example could be that s/he said s/he had experience in a certain required area. Later you found that s/he had little or no experience and are unsuitable because of it. S/he lied on the interview – and your notes will back you up.

    When there is a panel interview, decide who will ask each question. For instance:

    If it's a management position, one manager might ask questions relating to candidate's knowledge of management and leadership style.

    a) Using *'What if ...?'* examples: *'What if you have two employees who can't seem to get along, their work output is being affected – how would you handle this problem?'*
    b) Technical questions: *'When you make journal entries, what steps would you take?'*

    c) Ask candidate what kind of work environment s/he likes: large office, small office, prefer to work independently or be a member of a team?

2. Review each application carefully and jot down questions regarding the information submitted. If there were gaps in employment, etc. pursue these and find the answers.

3. Many resumes don't include enough information such as:

    (a) Salary of last position;
    (b) Supervisor (for reference) of last position;
    (c) Duties and level of position;
    (d) Reason for leaving. (Don't forget to ask this one!)

If the candidate had submitted only a resume, ask them to fill out an application form before the interview. Candidates would add only information not already on their resume.

Most application forms also require a signature from the candidate and many request permission to contact references. It's recommended that you have the following statement at the end of your company's application form:

Reference Permission Section on Employment Application Forms:

****

I certify that the statements made by me in this application and attached resume are true and complete. I understand and agree that a false statement may disqualify me from employment or result in dismissal.

Permission is granted for (your company name) to contact my past employers for references.

Date..

Signature..

■■■

Make sure they sign the reference permission section.

4. Provide proper surroundings for the interview.

    a. Cut off interruptions (telephone, personal assistant);
    b. Be punctual and organised;

   c.   Know the candidate's resume;
   d.   Know about the position you're recruiting for;
   e.   Be prepared to sell your company.

Employment interview questions:

What are employers really looking for when they hire an employee? They expect an honest day's work for a full day's pay. They want enthusiasm, a person who's working towards their chosen career goal and not just 'putting in time.'

A manager's strength comes from those they delegate work to. The quality of work produced by their subordinates either makes them look good or bad, because they're ultimately responsible for everything their subordinates do. The candidates must be able to show employers that they have these qualities.

The responsibility of the interviewers is to obtain the information they require to establish whether the candidate really has the requirements they're looking for.

Avoid asking questions that are not job related. These are questions relating to age, sex, marital status, birthplace, ancestry, religion and physical characteristics (unless directly related to the duties of the position). Stay away from questions about the applicant's views on family planning. If you're not sure whether you should ask a particular question, ask yourself whether your question is job related. If it isn't then don't ask it!

Here are some common job-related interview questions. Pick several then add other more job-related questions to your list.

1. What are your future career plans?
2. How do you spend your spare time? What are your hobbies?
3. What types of positions interest you most?
4. What jobs have you held? How were they obtained and why did you leave?
5. What do you know about our company?
6. What qualifications do you have that makes you feel you'll be successful in this position?
7. Do you prefer any specific geographic location? Why?
8. Do you prefer working with others or by yourself?
9. What kind of supervisor do you prefer?

10. Why do you think you'd like this particular type of position?

11. What personal characteristics are necessary for success in your chosen field? Do you feel you have these characteristics?

12. How did your previous employers treat you? (Watch for bad-mouthing or signs of discord or trouble).

13. What interests you about our product (or service)?

14. Do you like routine work?

15. What kind of people would you rather not work with?

16. Do you enjoy sports as a participant - as an observer?

17. What jobs have you enjoyed the most? The least? Why?

18. What are your own special abilities?

19. Do you prefer a large or small department to work in? Why?

20. Do you like to travel?

21. Is overtime a problem?

22. Have you worked with teams before? Work alone mainly?

23. Have you ever supervised others before? Under what circumstances?

24. Have you ever been fired from a position in the past? Why? (Is it possible they were asked to resign?)

25. What is your ultimate career goal? What steps have you taken to reach this goal?

26. What kind of energy level do you feel you have?

27. Are you a high, medium or low achiever?

28. Is your energy level higher in the morning, afternoon or evening?

29. What causes you stress in a work environment?

30. How do you relieve stress when it becomes a problem?

31. What kind of training do you feel you'd need if we offered you the position?

32. Why should we hire you? (Make sure you ask this one!)

33. What are your salary expectations?

34. How was your attendance at your last position? What were the main reasons for your absenteeism? (Watch for excuses about sick family members or chronic illnesses of their own.)

35. If I were to contact your former employer, what kind of a reference do you think they would give me? (This is one of my favourite questions, which often provides unexpected reactions from the candidate).

36. Tell me about yourself. (Candidates who answer this question by telling you their life story, miss out on the ideal opportunity to 'toot their own horn' that this question should encourage them to do).
37. When are you available for employment?
38. What are your major strengths? Again an opportunity for candidates to 'toot' their own horn.'
39. What are your major weaknesses? Some candidates may become completely flustered when asked to describe their 'weaknesses.'

Testing candidates

These tests could evaluate how well a designer can put ideas on paper, how fast a data entry person can type, a candidate completes accounting procedures or any other test that will determine whether the candidate has the knowledge you require to fill the position.

Other tests can be performed and evaluated by psychologists. Top management were the only people who were given these tests in the not-so-distant past, but these tests have proven so effective that many firms use them for all their applicants. A basic ability test evaluates personality, knowledge, reasoning, expanse of knowledge, ability to problem solve and measures preferences of work surroundings, their own personal style and their value systems, whether they're people or detail (results-oriented) driven. These are evaluated against a candidate profile that's been determined before the interviews were conducted. The candidate closest to the ideal profile gets the job.

Panel VS individual interviews

Single interviews (one interviewer) can be highly successful, providing the person knows how to interview properly.

I prefer panel interviews when the hiring manager(s) are not aware of proper interviewing techniques. One of the panel must be skilled at putting the candidate at ease. Most panel interviews include one person from the company's Human Resources Department, the manager of the position and possibly his/her manager.

The Human Resources representative normally asks general questions about the candidate's background, will watch that others on the panel don't ask illegal questions and explain company benefits to the candidate. Other panel members usually field questions regarding the objectives of the department, chances of advancement, what kind of group the candidate would work with and provide any technical information required.

During the interview:

To evaluate your candidate in the short time allotted, try the following:

1. Make sure there is adequate time to interview candidates properly. Put the applicant at ease. Be friendly and thoughtful. Shake their hand and introduce them to others on the panel. Don't play games such as purposely seating them so the sun is in their eyes and you're in shadow. Much communication goes on via eye contact and if you're in shadow, they can't read your expression.

    Another ploy some employers use is to seat the candidate in a chair that's off balance. The idea behind this is to keep the candidate mildly unsettled throughout the interview (I don't approve of this practice at all).

    Another game is that on panel interviews, the interviewers 'grill' the candidate thoroughly to try and make the prospective candidate extremely uncomfortable. Only when it's necessary for candidates to handle high degrees of stress on the job should this tactic be considered. These are all unfair tactics and are not encouraged during interviews of prospective employees.

2. Show by your manner, speech and facial expression that you're interested in them. Watch that your body language does not argue with your verbal language. You can show favouritism or dislike for another person, just by the way you sit, wiggle in your seat, pump your foot, tap the table, lack eye contact or gaze around the room etc.

3. Avoid showing disapproval, embarrassment or shock at anything that's said. Any sign of opposition will create a barrier.

4. Pause briefly after they answer your questions. This allows them the opportunity of amplifying their answer. Try it. Most people feel they must say more if you sit quietly looking at them.

5. Listen. You can't assess them when you're talking. Let the candidate talk 85 to 90% of the time except when you're explaining the position and duties to them (after you've learned what they have to offer the company).

6. Try not to ask questions that candidates can answer with a simple 'yes or no.'

7. Phrase questions so they're non-threatening. Example: Not: *'Why did you leave a good job like that?'* Say instead: *'How did you happen to leave that company?'*

   Don't be critical. Candidates should not have to defend their actions or opinions. You want to know what their actions have been and why, so you can make an accurate evaluation. Ask candidates to elaborate when necessary by repeating part of their answer (in a questioning tone).

   Example: Candidate: *'I don't think there's any future in the company.'*

   You: *'There isn't any future?'* (pause)

8. Avoid blunt statements:

   Example:

   Not: *'You don't seem to have set any career goals.'*

   Say instead: *'Have you had a chance to decide what you want to do in your career?'*

9. At the end of the interview, let candidates know when you'll be getting back to them (make sure you follow this). Then thank them for attending the interview.

Areas for in-depth probing

Before the interview, establish which questions you'll ask every candidate. Then add to this list any questions relating to their personal background. Areas where you may wish to spend extra time are:

Intelligence:

In addition to scholastic levels achieved, what can you discover about the applicant's range of knowledge? Ask specific, *'How would you deal with ...?'* questions.

Energy Level:
Does the candidate have the ability to sustain a high level of work activity? How has the candidate demonstrated this? You might have to check this area on your reference checks.

Forcefulness:
Is the candidate vigorous in the presentation and defence of opinions - or is the candidate merely defensive?

Perception:
How sensitive is the applicant to the feelings and motivation of others? Does the candidate reveal an awareness of his/her impact on fellow workers (consequences of actions)?

Interests:
Does the candidate have a wide range of interests other than work? Is there a reasonable grasp of current affairs? Does the candidate give the impression that s/he's a social butterfly or socially restricted?

Motivation:
Is work a source of personal satisfaction? Does the candidate want to achieve more than expected or is just 'getting by' good enough for them? Do they appear to be 'self-starters' or do they appear to need prodding to get the job done?

Stability:
Is the candidate resistant to stress or would a high stress situation affect his/her ability to perform? What are the candidate's comments about stress and the work pressure in his/her previous jobs?

Adaptability:
Does past performance show flexibility, such as an ability to change as an employment situation changes? Have they shown consistent growth in their past positions? Have they taken courses to keep them up-to-date in their knowledge? Was this training paid for by their company (forced training) or did they obtain the necessary training on their own?

Dependency:
Does the candidate have a normal need for approval from superiors; or is there a tendency to be excessively dependent on

other's opinions? Did they appear too independent and seem to buck the system or their manager's wishes?

Attitude:

What does the candidate think of previous employers? Did s/he identify with the company's corporate values and policies? Did s/he bad-mouth his/her former employers?

Leadership:

Has the candidate held a leadership position? Is it similar to the one for which you're interviewing? Has the candidate been responsible for hiring, training, motivating, doing performance appraisals and disciplining others? Is this important to the position you have open?

Decision-making:

Is the candidate systematic in his/her decision-making approach; or is there a tendency to play hunches and follow intuition or first opinions? Do they appear to need too much guidance? Do they appear too headstrong, likely to get themselves into trouble by not asking for help when necessary?

Organisation:

What in the candidate's history shows s/he's a well organised person? Can candidate plan effectively and carry out those plans? Does his/her background appear organised - show some continuity in it?

Communication:

Does the applicant communicate effectively with others? Does the candidate organise information before passing it on to others? Does s/he have the level of verbal fluency required for the position? Did s/he interrupt others or have trouble getting words out?

Objectivity:

How realistic were candidates in assessing their personal assets and liabilities - strengths and weaknesses? Were they realistic in the expectations they had of employers? Did they over- or under-estimate their abilities relating to the contribution they could make to your company?

Green/red flags

These are warning or attention signs relating to the candidate being interviewed:

Green flags: These are attention signs of good qualities in a candidate that you might miss if you don't follow-up.

For example:
You're looking for management experience. His work history shows that he's never held a management position before. You might overlook him as a suitable candidate unless you noted that he's the president of his community club (which involves management of the executive and others).

Or you may have noted that the candidate received an award at a university. Another candidate may say *'They were so pleased with my work, that I received two promotions within one year.'*

Don't miss the opportunity to ask questions relating to these pluses.

Red flags: These are signs of problems.

For example:

'My boss and I just didn't get along.' Or,
'They never seemed to use my ideas.' Or,
'I have trouble getting going in the morning.'

Ask questions to obtain more information about these possible problem areas.

Trouble signs to watch for:

To help you maintain a balanced overall view of the candidate in relation to the employment position, here are a few 'red flags' to look for; they should be investigated:

- They were late for the interview with little or no excuse.
- Came to interview looking unkempt, clothing wrinkled or soiled, hair not combed and generally looking very sloppy.
- Did they concentrate on such things as salary, company benefits, time off, vacations etc. rather than concentrate on the job itself?

- Are there indications of immaturity that could detract from work performance? Did they come to the interview with friends, relatives or their children? Look for the tendency to:
  o Blame others;
  o Are hyper-critical;
  o Are unable to make unpopular decisions;
  o Have unrealistic and over-blown claims of accomplishment;
  o Are hypersensitive to criticism;
  o Have aspirations beyond their ability;
  o Display irresponsible or over-demanding behaviour?
- Did they automatically light their cigarette without asking if they could do so or enquire whether they were in a non-smoking place of employment?
- Watch for signs of personal and emotional instability.
- Did they seem to know little or nothing about the function, service or product your company offers?
- Did they refuse to give you eye contact? (Many cultures encourage people not to give direct eye contact to someone in a position of power - you in this case. Don't over-react to this one.)
- Has the candidate changed jobs frequently for no good reason?
- Have there been frequent residence changes? Are there good reasons?
- Does candidate skirt around some questions, refuse to answer others without a sound reason?
- When asked the question: *'If I contacted this manager for a reference, what do you think s/he'd say?'* the candidate appears uncomfortable. Be sure to make a reference check on these issues.
- The talkative candidate that appears to have difficulty following the train of talk on an interview. The one who rambles on, has trouble remembering what question you asked or appears to like the sound of his/her own voice.
- The quiet one that's introverted - lacks verbal fluency. (When you may require someone to deal effectively with clients either on the phone or in person).
- The hyperactive person who has not learned how to channel his/her energy into constructive use.

- The person that appears to jump from one kind of profession or calling to another without any set career plan.

If you get the impression that 'something's not quite right' but you can't put your finger on it – that's your gut reaction or intuition working. I've learned to listen to this caution and usually follow-up with questions to their references that will confirm or deny my concerns.

What should interviewers guard against?

The first principle in understanding and evaluating others is to keep an open mind. What most interviewers see, hear and feel within the first four minutes of an interview often decides whether they like the candidate or not. Give the candidate a chance. Learn to evaluate them after you have all the evidence - not after four minutes!

It's possible that the candidate looks or acts like someone you don't like. This will affect your analysis of the skills of the candidate. It's also possible that you're rather a people person and this person is much more of a detail-oriented person. You may not be on the same 'wave length.' If this person is applying for a position in accounting, those qualities are probably ideal for the needs of the position. The person who appears aloof in the first four minutes may be using this as a screen to mask their nervousness.

Here are some tips to keep in mind when interviewing candidates. We as individuals have our own failings, so we must guard against the following:

1. Biases:

Snap judgements such as, *'Her red hair shows she has a temper.'* Or *'He looks dishonest.'* often results in the loss of a good potential employee. Sometimes we may be blind to our own biases and prejudices. This is why panel interviews are much fairer to the candidate. They're fairer to the company as well, because others will pick up information that you might miss on the interview. Take a few moments to determine what your biases and prejudices may be.

2. Halo Effect:

Don't form an overall impression (favourable or unfavourable) on the basis of one or two attributes. Poised and articulate people are not necessarily good managers. This can leave you vulnerable to impostors and con artists. Be sure to check references.

3. Projection Affect:

Don't put your own value system into the rating. People are unique. They differ from you and have the right to do so. The soccer enthusiast should not rate an accountant by his/her soccer prowess or knowledge.

4. Over-stressing Weaknesses:

We all have weaknesses and the interview will probably identify some. They may compensate for these weaknesses with strengths related to the needs of the job.

5. Insisting on too much directly related experience:

Most of the world's difficult jobs are held by people who had never done them before. Rigid specifications will remove many applicants that will leave you a much smaller pool of qualified candidates. Don't cut down your choices for good candidates.

Do you know what legal regulations you're to follow regarding employment or questions you can't ask on an interview? If you don't, you can no longer plead ignorance. As a manager, you must know and understand the laws that apply to hiring staff.

What can be asked on application forms and at interviews?

It's against the law to request unnecessary information that may be used later to discriminate is against candidates. It's important that employers take care with the questions they ask on application forms and on interviews. *The key is to ask questions that are directly relevant to the job.*

It's inappropriate to ask questions (either on application forms or during the interview) about the following:

- Marital Status;
- Sex and age;
- Number of children;
- Spouse's name;
- Country of birth;

- General health;
- Sick leave record;
- Religion;
- Criminal record;
- Sexual preference;
- Political affiliation;
- Union membership;
- Height and weight;
- Occupation of spouse;
- Workers compensation record.

For example:
If the job involves travel and/or regular overtime, ask all applicants whether they are able to do these things - rather than asking only the female applicants whether they will have to make arrangements for childcare and housework. Consider whether regular overtime is necessary or whether other arrangements could be made.

For instance it might be cheaper to hire someone part-time at a regular rate of pay rather than pay tired employees overtime pay with less return for their wages.

Race, colour, ancestry
An interviewer might want to know if a candidate's credentials are considered valid and/or equivalent in the candidate's new country. Candidates have the responsibility to obtain this equivalency information from a learning institute before attending interviews. If you're the interviewer, suggest that they do, but don't ask questions about their colour, race or where they obtained their education etc.

Next of kin:
The names of relatives or next of kin should not be asked in pre-employment inquiries as these can reveal the sex, sexual preference, marital status, place of origin or ancestry of the applicant.

Where a name is needed for purposes of notification in an emergency, the question should be phrased 'Person to notify in case of an emergency.' This information should be obtained *after* the employee is on staff, not at the interview or on the application form.

Dependents, Child Care:
Where applicable, valid inquiries would include willingness to work the required schedule, work overtime, to work rotating shifts, to travel or to relocate.

Questions often asked of women on interviews:

Don't ask illegal questions. If you find yourself tempted to ask one, determine the hidden motives behind the illegal question. Stay clear of what might be considered illegal questions such as:

'Who will look after your children while you're at work?'
'Who picks them up after school?'
'Are you married?'
'Are you planning on starting your family soon?'
'What country did you come from?'
'When did you come to our country?'
'Where does your spouse work?'
'What if your husband gets a transfer?'
'How old are you?'

If you're in the habit of using these kinds of questions on interviews, remind yourself that if the question isn't job-related - don't ask it. For instance, if you're interviewing a young woman (who you believe may have young children in day-care) you might be tempted to ask her:

'How old are your children?' Or,
'Who looks after your children while you're at work?'

If you asked yourself what you really wanted to know - you might say, '*This position requires that you be available with very little notice to work overtime. Would this cause you any difficulty?*' That's the question you should ask her - not about her children (which is illegal). If you ask her that question, you must ask all the male applicants the same question Or:

'There's a bit of travel with this position. Would your family object to that?'

57

The interviewer assumed that because she was a woman, she wouldn't want to travel because of family responsibilities. The question should concentrate on the real question which is, *'Can you travel on business if we need you to?'* Or,

> *'We'll be training you for this position which will take approximately six months, so we need to know if you can assure us of at least one years' employment in this position.'*

The last question would help you establish whether she's pregnant or if her husband's likely to be transferred in the foreseeable future. You might have the person sign a training agreement (See Chapter 6 - Training Agreements) that if s/he leaves the company within a specified period of time, s/he would have to reimburse the company for a portion of the training costs. However, all employees must sign such an agreement - not just the female staff.

Here's what I've advised candidates (who are seeking employment) to do when asked illegal questions. I ask them to determine what the interviewer really wants to know - then answer that unspoken question. So do ask the right questions. For instance:

Assumptions about women: Are not career-oriented - have limited desire for advancement.
Questions Asked: *'Are you married?' 'Are you thinking of starting a family soon?'*
What they really want to know is: *'What are your career plans for the next five years?'*

Assumptions about women: Have problems getting to work on time - working late or overtime when needed.
Questions Asked: *'Do you have any children?'* Or, *'Who looks after your children while you are at work?'*
What they really want to know is: *'What does your work record look like in terms of absences, lateness, etc.?'*

Assumptions about women: Are unwilling to relocate
Questions Asked: *'What does your husband do? Is he likely to be transferred soon?'*

What they really want to know is: *'Would you be willing to relocate?'*

Assumptions about women: Are unable to travel
Questions Asked: (Same as above)
What they really want to know is: *'Would you be willing to travel?'*

Assumptions about women: Lack required education and experience.
Questions Asked: Omission of related questions inquiring about these two areas.
What they really want to know is: *'How does your education and work experience relate to this present vacancy?'*

Assumptions about women: Quit too frequently.
Questions Asked: *'Are you planning on getting married soon?'* Or, *'Are you planning to start a family soon?'*
What they really want to know is: *'How long would you be willing to commit to this position?'*

Assumptions about women: Have little need for money.
Questions Asked: *'Why do you work?'* (Doesn't your husband make enough?)
What they really want to know is: *'What are your salary expectations?'*

Assumptions about women: Will not be accepted as a supervisor by men.
Questions Asked: *'Have you ever supervised men before?'* Or, *'Do you have problems getting along with male colleagues at work?'*
What they really want to know is: *'Describe your supervisory style.'*
Or, *'How would you handle a male subordinate who ...?'*

Assumptions about women: Unable to do strenuous physical work.
Questions Asked: Omission of related questions enquiring about this ability.
What they really want to know is: *'Have you been able to do ... in your past experience?'*

59

Assumptions about women: Cry frequently.
Questions Asked: *'Would you get 'upset' if ... happened?'* Or, *'What would you do if ...?'*
What they really want to know is: *'How do you handle stress?'*

Assumptions about women: Incapable of fact-based decision-making.
Questions Asked: (Omission of related questions).
What they really want to know is: *'Describe your decision-making style.'*

If you, the interviewer, insist on obtaining answers to these illegal questions or if the candidate is subject to a barrage of illegal questions, the candidate might state: *'Several of your last questions were illegal but I'd be happy to answer any job-related questions you wish to ask of me.'*

This shows how important it is to always ensure that questions on an employment interview always relate to what the person will do on the job, not on the applicant's personal life.

If you insist on asking these illegal questions, be prepared to receive a discrimination notice relating to the Anti-Discrimination Act especially if you do not hire the candidate.

Why are applicants rejected?

Companies reject applicants for a variety of reasons. Here are the major reasons employers reject candidates after the interview stage:

1. Poor personal appearance.
2. Overbearing, aggressive, conceited, superiority complex, know-it-all.
3. Can't express themselves clearly - poor voice, diction and grammar.
4. Lack of planning for career. No purpose or goals (women are bad at this).
5. Lack of interest and enthusiasm - passive, indifferent.
6. Lack of confidence and poise, nervous or ill at ease.
7. Failure to participate in outside activities (9 to 5 type of worker).
8. Overemphasis on money. Interested only in best dollar offer.

9. Unwilling to start at the bottom. Expects too much too soon for existing talents, abilities and knowledge.
10. Makes excuses - is evasive - hedges at unfavourable factors in his/her past history.
11. Lack of tact.
12. Lack of maturity.
13. Lack of courtesy, ill mannered, lacks empathy.
14. Condemnation of past employers.
15. Lack of social understanding.
16. Fails to look interviewer in the eye.
17. Limp, fishy handshake (women and men).
18. Signs of indecision or procrastination.
19. Sloppy application form or resume.
20. Merely shopping around.
21. Wants job only for a short time.
22. Little sense of humour.
23. Lack of knowledge of field of specialisation.
24. Little interest in company.
25. Emphasis on who one knows.
26. Late for interview without good reason.
27. Failure to express themselves clearly in a manner appropriate to the level of position applied for.

Transferrable Skills

Sometimes a person with an entirely different background might apply for a position with your company. You will probably automatically reject them as a possible candidate for a position. However, I urge you to 'think out of the box' and open your mind to the fact that they might be the perfect candidate. They might have the ideal transferrable skills you are looking for.

Transferrable skills are those skills you can take from one occupational field into another. For example: supervisory skills, interpersonal skills, aptitude with figures and scheduling skills are all transferrable skills. This will allows the person to attempt new careers and expand their horizons for employment.

I am a career counsellor and coach people on how to find their transferrable skills. They may see qualities that they may have overlooked. I ask them to complete the following to identify some of their transferrable skills:

Decide whether you:

1. Can do well
2. Can do
3. Would like to do well
4. Can't do well
5. Not interested

1. Moving your body

a) Using motor co-ordination - Being well coordinated when moving different parts of your body.
b) Acting quickly - Doing something fast when necessary.
c) Using stamina - Continually doing physically tiring work without becoming exhausted.
d) Using strength - Doing heavy work - lifting, pulling or carrying heavy things.

2. Paying attention to detail

a) Following procedures - Doing things exactly as directed. Completing tasks at the right time and in the right order.
b) Verifying - Checking numbers or written materials to make sure they're right. Checking the work of others.
c) Record keeping - Maintaining written records of money, objects, merchandise, things or facts.
d) Sorting - Sorting things in the right order. Putting things in the correct place or category.

3. Using your hands

a) Using your fingers - Being exact when you use your fingers to hold or move things.
b) Operating - Controlling, guiding or otherwise running tools, machines, vehicles, electronic devices or equipment.
c) Assembling - Putting things together.
d) Adjusting - Changing the settings on machines, devices, musical instruments or electrical equipment to improve their performance.
e) Building/constructing - Using tools / equipment to build or construct objects, buildings or structures.
f) Fixing/repairing - Fixing equipment, tools, machinery, appliances, etc.

4. Leading others

a) Making decisions - Choosing an action and accepting responsibility for the consequences.

b) Directing/supervising - Overseeing or managing the work of others and accepting responsibility for their performance.

c) Initiating - Taking the first step. Getting things started.

d) Confronting - Telling others something that they don't want to hear about their behaviour, habits, etc.

e) Planning - Developing projects or ideas through systematic preparation and deciding in which order and at what time events will occur.

f) Organising - Coordinating the people and resources necessary to put a plan into effect.

5. Using numbers

a) Counting - Determining how many items there are in one group.

b) Calculating - Using basic arithmetic; adding, subtracting, multiplying and dividing.

c) Measuring - Using tools or equipment to determine length, angle, volume or weight.

d) Estimating - Judging the cost or size of things. Predicting the outcome of an arithmetic problem before it's calculated.

e) Budgeting - Planning exactly how you will spend money. Deciding what merchandise to buy and how much to spend or how to get the work done at the lowest cost.

f) Using numerical reasoning – Understanding how to work with numbers or statistics. Using numbers to solve problems. Knowing how to read data and interpret statistics.

6. Using your senses

a) Using sound discrimination - Hearing slight differences in sound.

b) Using colour discrimination - Seeing small differences in colours.

c) Using shape discrimination - Seeing small differences in shapes and sizes, observing how things are alike or different.

d) Using depth perception - Accurately judging distance, judging how far away or apart things are.

7. Being creative

a) Visualising/imagining - Being able to form a mental image of concepts, objects, forms, drawings, models blueprints, etc.

b) Creating/inventing - Originating new ideas or inventing new ways of doing things.

c) Designing/displaying - Dealing creatively with spaces, products, objects, colours or images.

d) Performing/entertaining - Getting up in front of an audience or camera to entertain.

e) Improvising/experimenting/adapting; making changes or modifications to get the job done. Finding new and creative ways to accomplish tasks.

f) Drawing/painting/sculpting – Conveying feelings/thoughts through works of art.

g) Writing/playwriting/composing – Creating new and original materials to entertain or amuse.

8. Being helpful

a) Serving - Caring, doing things for others, providing a service upon request or when others are in need.

b) Treating - Performing a treatment to relieve a person's physical or psychological problems.

c) Co-operating - Working together with others to reach a common goal; working as part of a team to complete tasks.

d) Advising/counselling - Helping others cope with their personal / emotional / educational / family / career concerns by providing information or suggesting ways to solve their problems.

e) Teaching/training - Helping others learn how to do or understand something.

9. Communicating with others

a)   Reading - Getting information from written materials. Following written instruction on what to do or how to operate something.

b)   Writing - Using good grammar to make sentences and paragraphs that make sense. Being able to express oneself and explain things in writing.

c)   Talking - Finding it easy to talk to strangers in ordinary conversation settings.

d)   Speaking - In front of a group or audience.

e)   Listening - Listening carefully to whatever the other person is saying and responding appropriately.

f)   Questioning - Asking the right questions to get useful information from others or to help them gain insight.

g)   Negotiating - Bargaining with others to solve a problem or reach an agreement.

h)   Persuading - Convincing others to do what you want.

i)   Reading body language – Understanding what a person is saying non-verbally.

j)   Explaining - Being careful and clear when you're telling people about things, so that they can understand you quickly and easily.

10. Using logical thinking

a)   Investigating/researching – Gathering information in an organised way in order to establish certain facts or principles.

b)   Analysing - Breaking a problem into its parts so that each part can be dealt with separately.

c)   Synthesising - Putting facts and ideas together in new and creative ways - finding new ways to look at problems or do things, creating new ideas by putting old ideas together in a new way.

When determining the spec sheet for the vacancy, look at the above lists and try to determine which of the skills listed are required for the vacancy. Then compare those skills with the record of the person you think has no experience in your area.

This is also an invaluable tool to use in-house for those who are unhappy with the position they're filling, but are good employees. It might give them some insight into other occupations (that use their unique transferrable skills) that might be suitable for them, possibly within your company.

One woman, who came to me for career counselling was working as a nursing supervisor, but because she now had a young family, found she couldn't adapt to the shift work. She was worried that she wouldn't be able to find work in any other occupation. I helped her determine what her transferrable skills were.

These consisted of such things as:

- An ability to supervise others;
- A knowledge of scheduling (to give patients medication etc.);
- Highly honed interpersonal skills to deal with all kinds of people from uppity doctors to cranky patients;
- The ability to keep meticulously detailed reports;
- Able to remain calm in emergencies;
- Was physically fit; and
- Able to make decisions quickly.

These were talents that could be useful in many occupations. She just had to find out which occupation she wanted to try.

She admitted that one of her passions was ladies' fashions. After examining her transferrable skills, I advised her that if she obtained the necessary retail training, her existing transferrable skills could be used as follows:

- An ability to supervise others (her staff);
- A knowledge of scheduling (only she'd be scheduling the buying of stock);
- Highly honed interpersonal skills to deal with all kinds of people from upset clients to cranky staff;
- The ability to keep meticulously detailed reports (stock records, sales, bookkeeping);
- Able to remain calm in emergencies (possible robbery or fire);
- Was physically fit (would be on her feet most of the day); and

- Able to make decisions quickly (when buying stock, marking-down merchandise, taking returns).

I explained that she'd likely have little trouble obtaining a position in a ladies' fashion shop. She decided to obtain the retail training and eventually worked her way up to the position of regional manager of an international ladies fashion outlet. Her skills as a nursing supervisor prepared her very well for her new career. She just had to fill in the gaps with relevant training.

One fellow (a mechanical engineer) had been very successful in his field, but he had a nervous breakdown at the age of forty. He had met his goals, but suddenly realised he didn't like what he had become or what he was doing! Unfortunately, his father and brother were mechanical engineers, so he had decided to follow their lead. After counselling, he decided that selling would be ideal for him, but he was worried he'd have to take a drastic salary cut that would seriously affect his family's standard of living.

When asked what he would rather be doing - he replied, *'You'll think I'm nuts, because I couldn't possibly earn enough doing what I want to do.'* He went on to explain, *'I was walking through the major appliance section of a department store and found myself explaining to a couple the ins and outs of the refrigerator they were looking at. The salesman didn't seem to be able to answer their technical questions and it felt great that I could help them understand how everything worked. But I could never earn as much money as a refrigerator salesman as I do at my existing job.'*

It turned out that he was so close to his problem; he couldn't see that he would be invaluable to many companies. I had interviewed hundreds of engineers and knew he had a unique talent. Many engineers admit they have trouble communicating their ideas either orally or in writing, but this man's communication skills were exceptional. I suggested he contact several firms that produce and sell technically difficult mechanical products to ask them if they required a salesperson with his background. He did so and within a week, he had received five job offers – all worth more than his existing salary.

So keep thinking 'out of the box' and don't overlook excellent candidates.

CHAPTER THREE

AFTER THE INTERVIEW

After the interview:

1. Evaluate the candidates
2. Choose the top two candidates
3. Check references of both
4. Make verbal job offer to top candidate
5. Make written job offer to top candidate

Reference checks:

Many job applicants feel they have to beef up their credentials to compete against other fast-trackers who've put in time at prestigious companies. An overanxious applicant may even go so far as to exaggerate the facts to gain an advantage. It's up to you to catch these little white lies - or risk hiring someone who's under-qualified for the position. Double-check advanced degrees; question any holes in dates of employment; ask in-depth questions about any claims that appear exaggerated; and generally listen to your intuition. Follow-up on any area that causes you doubt.

The interviewer must make reference checks *before* the job offer is made! Information requested might include:

- Dates of employment
- Position held
- Duties of position
- Did candidate manage staff? (if relevant)
- Person and position reported to
- Salary
- How did candidate relate to peers, subordinates, clients and managers?
- How was employee's attendance and punctuality?
- How would you rate applicant's technical knowledge? Are there any problems or deficiencies?
- Quality of Work?
- Quantity of work?
- Personal grooming

- Dependability
- Cooperativeness

Important questions to ask:

1. What company did s/he work for before joining your company?
2. What company did s/he go to after employment with your company? (May point out gaps in employment)
3. Why did candidate leave your company?
4. Is there anything else you could tell me about the candidate?
5. Would you rehire? (This can tell you much more than most of the preceding questions. Always ask this one!)

Other questions would relate to concerns identified at the time of the interview. Be sure to note the date, name, position, company name, address and phone number of the person giving the reference.

Treat all reference checks as highly confidential

These are locked away in private files - not the employee's subsequent personnel file. Former employers may hesitate to say anything that might spoil the applicant's chance of earning a livelihood, even though his/her record with them may have been poor.

If former employers hedge with their answers - explain to them that the candidate has given you written permission. This is why it's imperative that you have candidates sign the release form on the bottom of your company application form.

Promise the person giving the reference that the information is strictly confidential and explain that you require their assistance in assessing the former employee honestly and without prejudice.

Sample Reference Check

[Company Logo]

Candidate details:
Candidate's Name:
Position Applied for:
Reference Check Conducted By:

Date of Reference Check:
Referee details:
Name & Position of Referee:
Employer/Company Name:
Referee Contact Details:
Candidate employment details:
(To be confirmed by Referee – Is the information provided by candidate correct?)
Job Title/Position Held: _____ Yes ___ No ___
Period of Employment: From _____ To _____ Yes ___ No ___
Salary at time of leaving (if relevant):
$_____Yes ___ No ___
Reason for Leaving: _____

Sample Questions:

- In what capacity have you worked with the candidate?
- Describe his/her working style. Provide examples of his/her communication organisation, productivity and work ethic:
- What level of supervision did s/he require?
- How quickly did s/he learn new tasks?
- How adaptable to change?
- Flexibility?
- How would you rate the quality of work performed?
  o Consistently high level?
  o Met job requirements?
  o Needed improvement?
- What were the candidate's strengths?
- What were the candidate's weaknesses?
- What were the candidate's developmental needs?
- How did the candidate deal with pressure/difficult situations?
- How did s/he relate to:
  o Peers?
  o Subordinates?
  o Clients?
  o Supervisors?
- How would you rate his/her punctuality / attendance?
  o Excellent?
  o Acceptable?

- o Below Average?
- How would you relate candidate's technical knowledge?
- Any problems or deficiencies?
- Would you re-employ the candidate? Yes __ No __ Why?

Additional Questions and General Comments:

Note: Replace the above questions with ones you feel might be more suitable so you can obtain the information you require to evaluate the candidate. In all cases, references must include a daytime contact number for referee. Mobile telephone numbers are unacceptable for this purpose.

Who should you contact?

Speak with the applicant's former supervisors. Those who have worked closely with a former employee know far more about his/her work habits than the Human Resources Department would ever know. Start with the last supervisor and work backwards. Check at least two, three if possible (if they are within the past ten years).

Problems may occur if candidates don't want to jeopardise their present position and may have been with their present employer for several years. Ask if there is a member or former member of the company who would comment on his/her performance (without endangering his/her position). There's considerable risk in hiring someone who won't agree to the above. References that are ten years or older don't normally warrant reference checks, unless there is only one employer during that time.

You've interviewed candidates, checked references and chosen the top candidate. What is the proper way of offering them a job?

The job offer:

First, make a verbal job offer either in person or on the telephone. Don't wait too long after the interview to contact the applicant or s/he may not be available. Speed is important here. Steps to take are:

1. Decide the salary you wish to offer.
2. Decide on the starting date.
3. Determine if you'll be offering relocation assistance if the candidate will have to move to take the position.

4. Make the verbal job offer.

If the candidate accepts the position:

5. Follow verbal offer with a written job offer.
6. Determine where the person will report on the first day.
7. On the formal job offer, include the following information:
   a) Salary;
   b) Start date of employment;
   c) Title of position they will hold;
   d) Where they report;
   e) Whom they report to;
   f) Probationary period (if there is one);
   g) Possibly mention when first salary increase will be;
   h) Welcome them to the organisation;
   i) Any other pertinent information (such as relocation information).

Note: A written job offer is equivalent to
a contract in a court of law.

Be careful what you put down. Think carefully. If there's a chance you might withdraw the job offer before the candidate's start date, don't send one.

Sample Job Offer (senior position in the company)

This is a job offer for a senior position in a company.

[Company Logo]

Private & Confidential

Date
Name of new employee
Address of new employee

Dear (Name of new employee)

I am pleased to confirm our offer of employment to the position of (Position) within (Company). Subject to clause 13, your appointment to this position will commence on (date).

We are happy to offer you employment within (Company) on the terms and conditions set out in this letter.

Terms and Conditions:

1. Position and Responsibilities

Your position will be (Position name). You will report to (Name and title of person).

The major responsibilities of your role are as discussed at the time of your interview and as shown in the attached Position Description.

2. Probationary Period

Your employment for the first three months is on a probationary basis. Before the end of the period of probation, your performance will be reviewed by your supervisor. Your employment with (Company) is conditional upon your satisfactory performance during the probationary period.

During the probationary period (Company) may terminate your employment by giving you two week's notice or payment in lieu of such notice. Similarly, you may terminate your employment during the probationary period by giving (Company) two week's notice.

In the case of serious misconduct during your probationary period, your employment may be terminated without notice.

3. Remuneration

In your role with (Company) you will be entitled to flexible packaging arrangements. Current packaging guidelines are available on the enclosed document. Please read these guidelines in conjunction with your employment contract.

Total Employment Cost: The Total Employment Cost (TEC) for flexible packaging purposes includes salary, all non-salary benefits and superannuation (including company and employee contributions). Your TEC is (Amount).

To ensure your package is implemented promptly, your initial remuneration package will be processed as salary and superannuation only. You will be sent a copy of this package shortly after you commence. If you wish to make changes to your package, please contact the administrator at (phone number) and s/he will be happy to asst you.

Your salary will be paid into a bank or building society account of your choice.

Some of the packaging options are as follows:

Motor Vehicle

You may elect to have a motor vehicle within your package. Motor vehicles are subject to policy as varied from time to time.

4. Superannuation

As an employee of (Company) you will now become a member of (Name of Plan). This is an 'accumulation' benefit fund and gives you flexibility and choice on how your funds are being invested. Details of (name of plan) and a member's kit will be available to you shortly.

Your total employer and employee contributions are charged to your package at a total rate of (percentage) of Superannuation Salary. Superannuation salary is calculated as (percentage) of your TEC.

It is intended that greater flexibility in setting the contribution rate at a level of your choosing will soon be available.

5. Remuneration Reviews

Remuneration is based on performance. The frequency of the review will be in line with (company) policy. Remuneration reviews fall due in January of each year.

6. Leave Provisions

Annual Leave

You are entitled to four weeks annual leave for each twelve months of service, including leave loading in accordance with policy. Staff are encouraged to take their leave as it falls due and not to accumulate more than four weeks annual leave at any point in time. In addition to your annual leave entitlement you will be entitled to two weeks leave without pay in each twelve months of service.

Long Service Leave

You will be entitled to thirteen weeks long service leave after fifteen years continuous service and to four and one third weeks long service leave for each completed five years of service thereafter. Pro rated long service leave is paid in lieu should you leave (Company) completing ten years service you may access all or part of the accrued long service leave as paid leave, provided that each leave is of at least four weeks duration.

(Company) policy is that long service should be taken in full within two years of the first thirteen week entitlement falling due and at a time agreed with your supervisor.

Parental Leave

You will be entitled to parental leave in accordance with policy.

Personal/Carer's Leave

Personal / Carer's leave will be available to you in accordance with policy. You are entitled to paid Personal / Carer's leave for absence due to:

a) Personal illness or injury
b) Family or household emergency
c) Death of an immediate family or household member.

7. Expenses

(Company) will reimburse you for any reasonable expenses you incur in the execution of your duties, upon production of receipts. Expenses covered include reasonable travelling, accommodation and other out-of-pocket expenses as required by (Company).

(Company) will pay any reasonable expenses you incur in relocating to (City). Expenses covered include reasonable travelling, removalist, accommodation and other out-of-pocket expenses. The amount of each such expense should be agreed by your supervisor prior to the expense being incurred.

8. Confidentiality Agreement

As an employee of (Company) you are not to use any confidential information (including intellectual property) and documents of (Company) for any purpose other than in the proper performance of your duties.

Your obligation to not to use any confidential information or documents continues after your employment ceases with (Company).

9. Termination of Employment

Should you decide to resign from (Company) you will need to give at least four week's notice in writing to your supervisor.

(Company) may terminate your employment at any time by giving you three months notice in writing or in the case of serious misconduct, your employment may be terminated without notice.

In the event of either party giving notice (Company) may, at its option terminate your employment immediately by making a payment equivalent to your total remuneration for the relevant notice period, less any applicable tax. On termination, you will also be paid any untaken accrued entitlements (e.g. Annual leave) in addition to any payment in lieu of notice.

In the event that your position becomes redundant and (Company) is unable to redeploy you to a suitable alternative position, you will instead receive a redundancy payment which will be determined in accordance with policy at that time. The redundancy payment will be no less than the remuneration for the notice period mentioned above.

On termination of your employment, you are required to return to (Company) any property which is in your possession or control, including confidential information, keys, documents, corporate credit cards and security pass.

10. Code of Ethics

(Company's) equal opportunity program aims to:

Ensure that its company policies and practices are non-discriminatory

Promote a positive and progressive environment that allows the company to attract and retain the best staff in an increasingly competitive environment.

(Company) believes it is the right of all staff to work in an environment free of harassment. Sexual harassment, which is a form of offensive behaviour and is detrimental to staff morale, is unlawful sex discrimination and constitutes unacceptable conduct in the workplace. It will not be tolerated under any circumstances.

You should also be aware that inappropriate usage of electronic mail contravenes the Discrimination and Harassment policy. Sending of offensive material through email may be construed as sexual harassment and (company) has adopted such a policy.

11. Occupational Health and Safety

(Company) aims to provide a safe, healthy and efficient work environment for all staff members. We are therefore committed to providing every staff member with a safe and healthy place in which to work and this is reflected in our work methods and work environment. We seek your cooperation in achieving this goal.

(Company) has adopted a smoke-free environment. You are not permitted to smoke in (Company) premises.

12. Criminal History Check (only if required)

We require a criminal history check to be undertaken by the police before an employee commences work with (Company). If the results of this check are not satisfactory to us we may terminate your employment without notice.

13. Your acceptance

Please confirm your acceptance of these employment terms and conditions by signing and dating the attached copy of this letter and return to me.

On a personal note (Name of Person), I look forward to you joining our team on (date). Please meet me in my office at 9:00 a.m. on that date. I am sure this role will provide you with significant opportunities to contribute very positively to the development of our company.

Sincerely,
(Name)
(Position)

Acceptance of Offer

I, (Name of Person) have received this letter dated (date) and accept the position of (Position name). In signing below, I accept the terms and conditions set out in this letter.

Signed:_____

Date:_____

(Note) A copy of the position description would be attached to this document

The first day:

Start your new employee properly. Formal orientation programs are a good first step towards integrating new employees into your staff. Because new employees usually learn the 'real' ropes from their peers, introduce him/her to the rest of the staff, then appoint an 'old timer' (usually long-term employee) or friendly workmate who 'adopts' the newcomer. This person acts as their guide.

Many new employees have questions they're afraid may sound stupid to their supervisor. They feel more at ease asking a workmate than asking their boss. The helper shows the new employee where the washroom is, when and where to go for coffee and lunch breaks and make them feel welcome with other workmates and lets them in on office politics. This takes the edge off the situation for the new employee in a way that the supervisor could not. It also introduces them to their new peer group. The supervisor's role is to set the atmosphere, then back off to let it work.

We all know how difficult it is the first two weeks on a new job. The supervisor should set up an appointment with him/her two weeks after s/he begins work so s/s/he can keep in touch with the new employee to see if there are any problems.

If supervisors are skilled at delegating and motivating employees, there should be little need for formal discipline. But if it's necessary, supervisors must be prepared to handle one of their most unpleasant duties - that of conducting disciplinary interviews.

CHAPTER FOUR

OTHER HUMAN RESOURCE DUTIES

Conducting proper Performance Appraisals is extremely important to the success of a company. This is an area where almost 95% of companies fail, mainly because they do not take the first step in establishing exactly what their staff are doing that they are evaluating. Their job descriptions are so vague and subjective that it would depend on the mood of the interviewer as to what kind of performance review the employee would receive on Performance Appraisal day. These kinds of performance appraisals have got to stop!

If things are done correctly, there are no surprises for the employee at performance appraisal time - no apprehension as to what they have and have not done correctly. This is because they and their supervisors have set concrete, measurable standards of performance for every task they complete. And the supervisor identifies problem areas as they occur - not waiting till performance appraisal time to pounce on their employees.

The employee is able to judge whether s/he did or did not meet those requirements. It also stops supervisors from making incorrect evaluations of what the employee is actually accomplishing - stops favouritism and bias on the part of the supervisor/interviewer as well.

Performance appraisals:

Does your company offer regular performance appraisals? What are these appraisals evaluating – the employees' actual performance or such things as:

- Judgement
- Initiative
- Attitude
- Interpersonal skills
- Conduct
- Reliability
- Customer relations
- Product knowledge
- Appearance

- Organisational ability
- Planning ability
- Quality of work
- Dependability
- Job knowledge
- Acceptance of criticism
- Responsibility level
- Motivation
- Persistence
- Independence
- Dedication

Do you think these kinds of performance appraisals are effective? Are they fair? They can't be - because they're subjective - not objective. That kind of an evaluation would depend on whether the evaluator got up on the right side of the bed or not. The employee wouldn't know what to expect at performance appraisal time.

Performance Appraisals should evaluate how well employees reach measurable objectives. Along the way, employees should know exactly where they stand and there should be no surprises at performance appraisal time. To be fair, supervisors must know how to set standards of performance upon which to evaluate their employees.

Copies of Performance Appraisals go to the employee, supervisor, personnel file and union representative (if applicable).

If you wish to use our copyrighted performance appraisal for your company, please contact:

Cava Consulting info@dealingwithdifficultpeople.info

Planning a Performance Appraisal Interview

1. Make Reference Notes to ensure that you keep track of all the relevant facts.
2. Make sure you have all required Backup Information. i.e.
    a) To deal with excessive absenteeism, you'd need attendance records;
    b) To commend an employee on exemplary work, you'd show examples;

    c) For a performance problem - you'd need examples of work done or production output.

3. Plan the Sequence of the interview. Make sure you know the questions you need to ask to gain the necessary information. Which first - bad or good news?

4. Ensure Privacy. This is of utmost importance because the employee will feel far more comfortable and open if s/he can speak freely without being faced with worries of interruptions or other people over-hearing the conversation.

5. Allow enough time to properly conduct interviews. Unexpected information may surface and you might need more time.

6. Decide where the interview should be held. Choose the proper environment that's the least threatening to the employee. This could be at the employee's work station (provided there's privacy) in a neutral area such as a cafeteria or lastly, in your office.

7. Provide an atmosphere conducive to helping the employee improve. If employees believe they are 'in the hot seat' they'll automatically feel defensive. The main focus of interviews should be to help employees improve their performance – not to bring on retaliation from them.

8. Be open to new ideas. Your employees are the ones who are actually doing the job and often can come up with innovative, creative ideas about how their jobs can be conducted easier, faster and be more streamlined. You won't hear their ideas unless you provide an atmosphere that shows you're ready to listen.

9. At the end of the interview, be sure to ask, *'Is there anything that I can do to make your job easier?'*

Why are Performance Appraisal Meetings Held?

The major purpose of a performance appraisal meeting is to discuss and resolve differences so you and the employee can agree on the final appraisal of his/her performance. Also:

a) To determine who your effective employees are by accurately and fairly measuring individual employee results and accomplishments.

b) To constructively guide your employees' performance and improvement by:

    i. clarifying what, when, where and how employees are to perform assigned tasks by establishing fair and equitable standards of performance

    ii. having targets to shoot at, how much, how often, how well, etc.

c) To provide both positive and negative feedback to the employees relating to their ability to meet set standards of performance and recognition for improvements made.

d) To identify employees' strengths and weaknesses and determine ways to improve their behaviour and performance.

e) To ensure that employees have had the required training to accomplish assigned tasks.

f) To provide unbiased and valid decision-making in areas of compensation, performance correction, promotions, training and development, transfers and retention/release.

How to provide the right climate

1. Keep brief notes during the year to remind you of items you wish to discuss at performance appraisal time. Performance appraisal should be on-going. High quality work should receive recognition immediately and later on Performance Appraisals. However, if there's a problem, it must be discussed at the time of the problem - don't wait till appraisal time to 'dump' on the employee.

2. The actual performance appraisal discussion consists of sharing of ideas between the supervisor and the employee being evaluated. Supervisors who merely present their evaluations in lecture form, thwart their success in two ways:

   They learn little about their employee, who knows the most about their performance. Supervisors who listen more than talk will have more useful information to work with and can end the discussion with a better understanding of the employee's performance, strengths and developmental needs.

   They limit employee commitment to the performance improvement plan. Employees will act favourably upon a plan they help develop - not one to which they didn't contribute.

3. Supervisors shouldn't insist on running the meeting according to their own agenda, but encourage employees to disclose their views about performance during the period under review. Often the items supervisors want to discuss are brought up by the employees themselves.

4. Good communication skills are a must. Too often people assume they know what the other person means. Learn to paraphrase to check out anything that might be misinterpreted. Use such statements as, *'As I understand it, you're saying ...'* and, *'So, if I hear you correctly you ...'* Watch for nonverbal clues - frowning, raised eyebrow, arms across the chest defensively, a smile. If an employee's body language seems to contradict their conversation, check to see whether they're getting your message correctly.

5. The questions supervisors use are important to invoke employee participation. Such questions as, *'What projects have you had problems with during the last performance period?'* can get the discussion on track. Don't put the employee on the defensive where s/he must defend his/her actions.

    Saying such things as, *'You couldn't have obtained that information from reliable sources!'* Instead, ask, *'Could you explain where you obtained the information you used to complete this report?'* or *'Where did you obtain the three estimates to come to your final decision?'*

6. Most people become defensive when they're put on the spot. Be ready to back up your evaluation with facts which will leave you less vulnerable to attack. If temperatures rise, call a 'time out.'

7. Focus on the behaviour of the employee by giving examples and stay away from personal opinions. Ask yourself, *'What events led me to make this evaluation?'*

8. Effective supervisors are willing to confront employees. For instance, *'We've talked several times about the importance of well-organised, reports. It bothers me that your reports continue to lack the proper information.'* S/he should identify specific performance s/he wishes

improved. These could be mixed in with positive evaluations:

'When you presented your report on the Miller account, the fact that you divided it into several sections made it easy for me to follow your thinking.'

'I was uncomfortable with your approach when you told Joe to 'shape up or ship out.'

'Thank you for being so patient when you explained our Policy and Procedures manual to Bill.'

'Because you finished your report in less than a day, it contains many errors. I'm concerned about whether you're rushing projects and not taking enough time planning your day.'

9. Stay clear of open-ended questions that can be answered by 'yes' or 'no.' Examples of how you can encourage input from your employee are:

    'What approaches do you think we should take to eliminate this problem?'

    'Tell me what you think about ...'

10. Emphasise employee's improvement rather than criticism. Instead of saying *'You made a mistake.'* Say, *'In the future I'd like you to do it this way ...*

11. Encourage the employee to suggest areas they believe require improvement which might be achieved through training.

12. The supervisor should be familiar with most aspects of the employee's performance and be ready to discuss these during the interview. When relying on information from others, it can be easy to obtain false impressions. Be willing to discuss particulars with employee.

13. Both supervisor and employee should prepare for the meeting with items they wish to discuss during the interview.

14. Whenever possible prepare the performance appraisal on a word processor yourself. When confidentiality is not assured, performance appraisals should be completed legibly by hand.

15. When setting objectives, make sure the employee has a clear understanding of what s/he is supposed to do.

16. Stick to the facts - don't use assumptions, guesses and use such statements as, *'I think ... I feel ... or I believe ...'* unless you're willing to back these statements up with facts.
17. Avoid evaluating all employees 'down the middle.' By doing so, you'll not be fair to top and bottom performers.
18. Employees are more likely to improve when they themselves recognise the need to improve, agree on a specific method of improving and are kept informed of their progress to meet specific needs.
19. Have employee share the interview by asking such questions such as:

'How do you see this?'
'What do you think?'
'I'm interested in your view.'
'Where do you think you can improve?'
'What training do you feel you need?'
'How do you think we can overcome this problem?'

Good or bad news first?

Should you begin your meeting with good or bad news? I recommend doing an overview first, *'I have been very pleased with your performance this past year.'* Then go right to the areas that require improvement. If you keep talking about what they've done correctly, they will be waiting to hear one word ... *'but'*... and won't hear a word you say that praises their work. Leave the praise till the end of the meeting.

Levels of Performance

The evaluation should be written so that an employee knows how s/he is performing in each area and where improvement is required. For example, your standards might be determined by the following criteria:

Outstanding performance
- Consistent and exceptionally high degree of accomplishment.
- Outstanding performance and contributions.

- Clearly represents the very best in the position.

Exceeds Requirements
- Performance and results consistently meet and frequently exceed job requirements.
- Generally fully accomplished.
- Clearly above standards of accomplishment.

Meets Requirements
- Meets performance standards given time and experience in position.
- Fully competent performer.
- May exceed job requirements occasionally.

Below Requirements

- Generally meets, but occasionally performs below standards of accomplishment.
- Improvement is desired in some areas. (You would need to identify these areas with time-frames for improvement.)
- May need further development due to being new in the position.

Inadequate
- Unsatisfactory performance
- Frequently below standards
- The need for improvement is serious and immediate (May be a probationary situation.)

How often should performance appraisal be completed?

Companies should conduct performance appraisals when employees complete their probationary period. After that, it can be done once a year - usually on the employee's anniversary date. Other companies conduct performance appraisals at the same time for every employee. Another company may have performance appraisals for each large special project their employees may complete (for example engineering or accounting firms).

Lee Iacoca asserts that all employees should have a performance appraisal quarterly. He believes that putting details down on paper makes a supervisor be more specific. It also assists a supervisor to:

1. Allow the person to be his/her own boss - to help set his/her own goals.
2. Make employees more productive and motivated.
3. Encourage new ideas.
4. Keep people from being buried or lost in the system.
5. The good guys don't get passed over.
6. The bad guys don't get to hide.
7. It improves communication between the supervisor and employees. The more employees set their own goals, the more likely they will react positively. If they don't measure up, the employee knows they've failed before the review. There are no surprises. Employees are often their own worst critics.

Who should conduct Performance Appraisal Interviews

Only the direct supervisor, foreman or manager of an employee should conduct a Performance Appraisals on that employee.

Supervisors in your company should have all of the following responsibilities:

1. Delegate work to subordinates
2. Check subordinate's work

Most supervisors and foremen have these two responsibilities, but unfortunately some don't have the next two:

3. Conduct performance appraisals
4. Discipline subordinates

Another responsibility that's an advantage is:

5. Hires own staff

If your Supervisors or Foremen have only the first two responsibilities, you've placed them in a 'lead hand' position. This is a 'no-win' situation for both supervisor / foreman and the employee. Do not put your staff into that kind of no-win situation

– it's too frustrating for the supervisor and allows employees to disobey the supervisor without the chance of being disciplined. Please check all job descriptions in your company to ensure that you are not doing this to any employee.

What information should be on an employee's personnel file?

- Job description
- Application Form and/or Resume or CV
- Copy of Job offer
- Copies of Performance Appraisals
- Written Disciplinary Warnings
- Health information (obtained after s/he's hired)
- Company pension information
- Superannuation
- Driver's licence information (if it is a requirement of the job)
- Educational confirmation
- Apprenticeship certificates
- Family, next of kin (emergency contacts)
- List of training received
- Training Agreement (see Chapter 6 for more on this topic)
- Security / police checks (if required)

What would you do if an employee asked to see his/her Personnel File? You must show it to them within 24 hours. There should be no surprises in their file – they should have copies of everything in it. Therefore - do not - and I repeat do not - put anything into an employee's personnel file that slants at discrimination such as 'cute blond,' 'hunk,' 'obese' or anything relating to their race or ethnic background.

The employee would be able to copy anything in the file but will not be left alone with it (in case s/he removes any damaging reports such as performance appraisals or written disciplinary warnings.)

Human Resources Policies and Procedures

Companies have policies and procedures relating to many facets of the work done by employees such as Operations, Traffic, Sales, Customer Service, Safety and Production. The head of the

Human Resources department is in charge of those that pertain to Human Resources.

A Policy:

Is a statement about an issue in the workplace and says what the business intends to do about the issue. For policies to be successful in the workplace, all employees affected by them must know about and understand the policy.

A Procedure:

This gives step-by-step instructions on how to deal with an activity in the workplace. Procedures need to be tested thoroughly before they are implemented. Employees involved in the procedure must clearly understand and be able to follow the written procedures.

Employment law is constantly changing. It's important that you check your Federal and State laws to adapt your policies, procedures, regulations and forms to meet the demands of those laws. Also be sure you're aware of any Enterprise and Union Agreements that affect the employees of your company.

Employee Handbook

Your company Employee Handbook should cover all the rules and regulations that an employee is expected to know and follow. They are an employee's guide that explains a company's rules and regulations. On the first day of the person's employment, s/he is given a copy of the company Employee Handbook to keep and after a week is asked to sign an agreement stating that s/he has read the handbook and understands its content.

This way both employees and employers are protected. The employee will be protected because s/he will know the company rules and regulations. The employer will be protected because if the employee breaks any of the company rules and regulations s/he won't be able to claim innocence if s/he has confirmed that s/he knew and understood the content.

Employee Handbooks normally back up a company's formal Human Resources Policy and Procedures Manual, so the first step is to produce the policies and procedures and move on to completing an Employee Handbook.

If you require assistance in producing either your company's *Human Resources Policies and Procedures Manual* or your *Employee Handbook*, you can obtain help from Cava Consulting by going to:

www.dealingwithdifficultpeople.info/consulting.htm

CHAPTER FIVE

MOTIVATION

Now that you've hired the right staff member, you'll need to know how to motivate him or her to bring out the best performance possible.

Motivation:

The expression 'different strokes for different folks' fits motivation as well. However, you may not be able to motivate some employees at all. Identifying the wants and needs of employees is a major task faced by most supervisors and Human Resources personnel.

> **Motivation like bathing must be done on a regular basis to be effective.**

Don't let employees use negative terms to describe what they do for your company. For instance, *'I'm only a receptionist ... janitor ... clerk, etc.'* Explain why their position is crucial to the smooth running of your company. Give examples of what the repercussions would be, if they failed to complete their tasks properly.

'Do you know how important you are to this company? You're the first person most of our clients speak to. If you answer the phone incorrectly or pass the messages on to the wrong person or delay doing so – we would lose many of our clients. So please don't think that you are not important to this company.'

'Could you imagine what a mess this department would be in if you weren't there to make sure it was presentable every day and to clean up messes we make during the day? You're very important to us and we appreciate what you do every day to keep things running smoothly.'

What motivates most employees?

Each employee has a different set of values and priorities. Try to hit their 'hot button,' then watch the difference in their performance. As different jobs attract different people, motivation is often very personal to an individual. Here are many that you could choose from, depending on the employee you're trying to motivate. See how many you've observed in the workplace.

Money.

Many feel this is the only thing that would really motivate employees. For some this is true, but for the majority, not true. Often the opportunity of making more money can be a motivator (possible promotion).

Recognition.

This is probably the best motivator of all. It's very high on employees' lists of things that truly motivate them. Recognition for a job well done seems to be the incentive for more favourable behaviour that in turn allows them to receive more recognition. A well-timed pat-on-the-back can turn around even the most lethargic, aggressive or demanding employee. If you want even more impact, put your praise down on paper, so the recipient can save it and read it whenever s/he wishes.

Seniority.

Employees receive special company benefits because of long-term employment. This could be a bigger office, more company benefits, a company car, etc. Unfortunately, this can de-motivate other more conscientious or high-achieving employees who see seniority as a negative reason for recognition and giving more money to those who have not earned it.

Merit System.

This would make sure that employees would receive a salary related to their productivity, rather than their seniority in their company. This eliminates much of the 'deadwood' in corporations. Those who've always expected their company to protect their employment simply because they've worked for the company for a long time, fear this method.

Status.

This would be in the title of the position or the employee's perceived importance to the company. For instance, would you prefer the title Junior Clerk or Input Worker? I'm sure you'll agree that Input Worker sounds much more important. An employee is less reluctant to give his/her title, if they were asked, *'What do you do for a living?'*

Challenge.

The opportunity to grow, to stretch, to use their full potential is the motivator for many. The idea of winning is a definite turn-on to many who enjoy the gamble.

Competition.

To those with a competitive nature (most sales types) competition is a definite turn-on to higher productivity. They thrive on the excitement of the challenge.

Security.

For employees who believe their jobs are in jeopardy (or those waiting for a pending lay-off) letting them know that their job is secure (and the company is solvent) may be the only motivator they need to do a good job.

Lack of Security.

If your job is on the line because of poor productivity or behaviour, they'll likely clean up their act and produce more (shape up – or ship out procedure). This is a negative motivator, but may be the only motivator for your lazier employees or those who lack direction and goals.

Responsibility.

Doing only part of the job, can be a turn-off to employees. When employees have the full responsibility for the completion of a task, they feel a much higher sense or achievement. They say, *'I was the one in charge of **that** project. I was so pleased when my boss said I did a good job.'*

Training.

When companies give training to their employees, staff feel as if their companies care about them and are interested in their well-being. Companies that utilise manpower planning will use training to make sure their existing staff are ready for promotional opportunities. They encourage development of talents and abilities and allow employees to use their training and experience.

Promotional Opportunities.

This is a turn-on to the high achiever or someone who really wants to get ahead in a hurry. For those who are at the minimum wage level, it can be an incentive to work harder, so they can earn more money.

Achievement.

Many companies make public announcements when their employees accomplish something unexpected. *'I'd like to congratulate Bill Martin who was able to obtain XYZ Company as a client. We've been trying to obtain this prestigious client for many years and Bill was able to pull it off. Congratulations Bill.'*

Awards.

Companies give perfect attendance awards, sales awards, charity awards and give recognition for work above and beyond the call of duty.

Extra privileges.

Employers might decide that employees can go home when they complete their allotted work.

Additional benefits.

This could include a company car, expense account, a corner office, own personal assistant, stock options, company credit card, season's tickets to concerts or sporting events or the use of a condominium in Hawaii, etc.

Leadership style of supervisor.

A good leader can motivate employees to give their best effort, simply because they respect their leader and want to do their best for him/her. In return they want their supervisor to be proud of them.

Hours of work.

Companies that implement flex time find it to be a great motivator. Their early risers (morning people) could start at 7:00 am and leave at 3:00 pm. Late starters would start work at 10:00 am and leave at 6:00 pm.

Job sharing.

This occurs when two employees share the responsibilities of one (normally full-time) position. Some split the duties with one person working in the morning, another in the afternoon. Salaries and benefits are also split in half. In other cases, the employees may work two days one week and three the next. It's an ideal set-up for working mothers, those with second jobs or those close to retirement.

Company Social Events.

The opportunity for workers to associate with each other socially is a good motivator for some employees. This could be having a company baseball team, bowling night, company picnic, barbecue or other social event.

The work itself.

Job rotation often reduces the boredom of repetitive kinds of tasks. There's another spin-off benefit - that of having more than one person qualified to take over the duties of a position. If an employee is on vacation or ill, another can take over his/her duties and stops any backlog.

When supervisors know the talents and abilities of their staff, they can delegate work to those who appear to like that kind of task.

Giving employees new tasks that keep them learning, will also remove the tedium of their work.

Supervisors should resist hiring either over- or under-qualified staff. Over-qualified staff will likely be bored with their job within months. If you've made this faux pas the employee will probably want a promotion in a hurry. You may lose them to another company unless you allow them that opportunity. Under-qualified staff will be playing the game of 'catch-up' which could be very stressful for them.

You'll need to give them extra training and time to catch up with the position expectations. Consider extending their probationary period longer than normal, so you have more opportunity to see if they can handle the position before making them permanent employees.

Working Conditions.

This is very high on the list for many employees. Anything you can do to make working conditions better, will repay your company's investment with increased productivity and higher employee morale. There are many things that companies can do to improve working conditions:

Lighting - either too much or too little.

Far too many offices have four bars of fluorescent lights in one spot. This is far too many. When there are this many lights together, it provides a glare that is extremely hard on the eyes, often causing eyestrain and/or headaches. Employees are squinting their eyes by late afternoon. This glare is similar to sitting in a boat on a bright sunny day without sunglasses.

The fluorescent light hits light surfaces (such as white paper) and reflects upward into the eyes of the worker (like the water does in a boat). Many employees have to wear tinted glasses to cut out the glare. A more sensible solution is to remove two of the fluorescent tubes. Even better - replace them with two orange-coloured soft fluorescent bulbs rather than the white ones.

When under stress, the pupils dilate (so the person can see the beast that's stalking them better) and their hearing becomes much sharper.

Noise.

If employees are working against deadlines, they're likely under some stress. This is why (when you're under stress) you jump when someone makes a loud noise and why companies try to reduce noise. These efforts include installing rugs, placing acoustic tiles in ceilings, use raised wall-coverings (such as matted wallpaper) and provide fabric-covered dividers between work stations. They turn telephone bell levels down or provide soft background music.

Anyone who's under stress suffers from the 'fight or flight syndrome.' This is their instinctive behaviour when under stress that prepares them to fight their way out of a predicament or to run away. When this happens, our five senses (including hearing) become far more sensitive.

Working position.

Standing.

Those who have to stand for long periods of time should have something to rest one of their feet on, which alternates the weight-bearing leg. At one time grocery store clerks could only work three to four hours at a time. Their employer believed that the lifting of articles and the packaging of groceries was the reason.

When one of the large grocery stores had their cashiers stand on half-inch rubber mats, they found they could work for much longer. The same concept was used where employees moved back and forth along a long counter. Companies find that employees' back and leg problems are drastically reduced. Because most businesses have concrete floors with no resiliency, the provision of rubber mats or rugs with deep underlay affords this same benefit.

Sitting.

Watch most employees when they're deeply engrossed in what they're doing. Most of them sit on the edge of their chairs. This doesn't let them take advantage of the back-saving support of their chairs. Make your staff aware of what they're doing and remind them to use this support.

Companies should condemn most secretarial chairs. Have you ever sat in one? Try leaning back. What happens? Right - you would probably tip the chair over backwards along with yourself. This is ludicrous when you figure the hours most support staff spend in those chairs. Companies should provide them with the same kind of chairs with arm rests their bosses have, only smaller to fit into the narrower space most have at their desks. They should be able to rest their arms on the armrests of their chairs which should be parallel with their desks. This way, they will have adequate support (especially for the hand that controls the mouse of their computer.)

Word Processors/computers.

Word processors and computers can cause not only neck strain but also eye strain if they're placed in the wrong position. The screen should be set at a comfortable height. Employees should not be looking upward towards their screen, but rather their eyes should be almost parallel with the top of the screen.

Be observant of the lighting around the screen. If there's a window behind the worker, it will reflect glare on the screen. The employee's eyes will then have the double problem of adjusting to the reflected light and the information shown on the screen. This is also true if light is hitting or reflecting on the screen from either side.

If there happens to be a window behind the screen, the worker's eyes will again be in trouble because of the direct light coming from the window. The ideal situation is to have light barriers set up in such a way that the screen has no reflected light at all. Providing non-glare screens is a definite asset.

Proper temperature.

Most offices have a constant battle between the male employees who wear heavy wool suits and the female employees wearing lighter apparel. Often men want the office cooler and women want more heat. Unless the working environment is comfortable for all workers, they may not be as productive as they should be.

Colour.

Colour has a definite bearing on the ability of staff to do a good job. One warehouse had all the walls and shelving painted grey. Their employees' moods seemed to match. They decided to re-paint their walls a creamy yellow and their shelves a different colour for each section.

It was soon apparent that this made a definite difference in the productivity and morale of their staff. It was also easier to find products because of the colour coding, *'It's on the third shelf of the blue shelving.'*

Plants.

These provide a soothing atmosphere and soften the glare of concrete and steel.

Furniture.

Wooden furniture appears softer, more pleasing and less serious than steel.

Maslow's Hierarchy of Needs

Mazlow's Hierarchy of needs can be very effective to help you motivate different employees:

Physiological Needs:

These include the fundamentals of survival, including hunger and thirst. Until this need is met, the four others won't likely be motivators. Money (or the lack of it) is what motivates most at this level.

High absenteeism and turnover are the results when these needs are not met. Proper temperature, tolerable noise level and a comfortable body position are more important as a motivator at this level than any other.

Supervisors might not be able to provide more money to their staff, but they can motivate employees by giving them recognition for a job well done and making them aware of promotional opportunities. Improving working conditions will likely help these employees do a better job and job rotation can help alleviate boredom.

Social Needs:
This is the yearning to belong, to have friends and acquaintances, to be liked and accepted. Supervisors need to take steps to make newcomers feel part of a group. Employees who work in a hostile atmosphere, seldom use teamwork when completing tasks, so supervisors must be on top of personality clashes. Many companies fill this need by providing social events for their employees to enjoy and socialise with each other.

Security Needs:

This is the need for safety. The employee wants to continue his/her physiological needs, but seeks protection against danger, illness and loss of his/her job or other threats to security. If a person feels his/her job in the company is in jeopardy, s/he will stop taking risks - will walk the middle-line and become an average or poor performer.

Supervisors must be on top of this situation and deal with conditions that appear to threaten the security of their staff. If staff fear a pending lay-off (and none is imminent) make sure they know this is not going to happen. If your staff is afraid of being replaced because of new technology - allay their fears about being replaced. Keep aware of their anxieties and try to alleviate them as soon as possible. Be proactive – not reactive.

Those who have obtained written warnings on their file will feel their security is threatened. They'll stop taking risks and may give only average performance (even though they're capable of much more).

Non-smokers forced to work in an environment that allows smoking, object to the security risk to their health. Many will leave a job because of this lack of security and safety.

When employees have met their physiological and security needs, others surface.

Ego Needs:

This is the need for self-esteem and recognition received from others. To these individuals, status level is important; where the title of their position might be important - even more important than salary.

Employees must feel that others respect them and want their efforts recognised. If they're not, they'll channel their energies elsewhere (Possibly they'll become a star bowler - expending more energy at social things). If supervisors channel this energy towards more productivity, they'll likely improve the ego of the employee as well.

Self-Actualisation:

Freed from the difficult task of satisfying external needs, people are now ready to explore their true selves. They can use their interests, talents, skills, knowledge and abilities to fulfil their highest potential as human beings.

Everyone benefits if a supervisor can get an employee to this level by meeting his/her motivational needs. This is why it's important to find your employee's 'hot button.' It's unfortunate, but approximately 80 per cent of all employees are in the wrong job! You'll believe this if you ask people about their jobs. The ones who are happy (self-actualised) will describe their job in positive terms. Those who aren't self-actualised will use negative terms to describe what they do.

If a company doesn't recognise and use the potential of both its high and low achievers and attempt to motivate people, their employees may simply move elsewhere. Many find that they can only reach this level by being self-employed where they can use all their talents and abilities. A supervisor can provide this atmosphere by making employees feel as if they're working for themselves. Companies that offer stock options believe their employees feel more important. What they do on the job affects them directly, so their performance improves.

Altruism:

This is the stage after self-actualisation where the person's content to see him or herself self-actualised, but wants others to reach this level as well. They usually forget competition and concentrate on developing the talents of others with little or no thought of pay. Many become mentors for junior staff who show promise.

Other examples of this are the auto mechanic who fixes his friends' cars in his spare time. Or the hairdresser who looks after the hair needs of all her friends. They love their job so much that they like to share their talents in their free time as well.

The Need Hierarchy at work:

Here's how you can motivate people at the different levels:

Physiological needs:
- Pleasant working conditions;
- More leisure time;
- More luxurious personal property;
- Avoidance of physical strain or discomfort; and
- More money as a means of providing basic comforts.

Social needs:
- Friendly colleagues;
- Opportunity for interaction;
- Harmonious interpersonal relations; and
- Team membership.

Security needs:
- Fringe benefits;
- Safe working conditions; and
- Seniority protection.

Ego needs:

- Opportunities for advancement;
- Recognition based on merit (not seniority);
- Job assignments that allow display of skill;
- Inclusion in planning activities; and
- Status related to job title.

Self actualisation:

- Involvement in innovative and active activities;
- Greater ego involvement;
- Increased investment of oneself in work; and
- Freedom to make one's own decisions.

Herzberg's Theory:

Dr. Frederick Hertzberg has explained Maslow's theories and places emphasis on motivation. He identified two sets of factors that affect the way in which people react.

Hygiene Factors: Fall under Physiological and Security levels - Pay, benefits, working conditions, fringe benefits, supervision, interpersonal relations, rules and policies.

Motivators: Fall under Social, Ego Status and Self Actualisation - challenge, responsibility, recognition, achievement, opportunity for personal growth, advancement and the work itself.

The hygiene factors don't help a person to move past an average performance level. True motivators are those that cause a person to be happy with their jobs and thus more productive. These are added to the hygiene factors so employees can move out of the average performance level.

Unsatisfied needs are strong sources of de-motivation in the work place. Supervisors should watch for these needs. By knowing their employees well, they'll learn what motivates each of them.

De-motivating Factors

Restrictive Supervision:
If you don't let your staff take an active part in how they complete their assignments, they're likely to obtain less job

satisfaction. The more employees participate in how they do things, the more co-operative they'll be.

A supervisor that uses an authoritarian leadership style all the time is setting him/herself up to fail.

Lack of Recognition:

Supervisors de-motivate staff if they identify only the 2 per cent their subordinates have done wrong, instead of concentrating on what the 98 per cent they've done correctly.

In the old 'School of Management' supervisors believed it was their right to take credit for ideas suggested by their subordinates. As expected, this just de-motivates employees and discourages any new ideas. Progressive supervisors know that if they give employees credit where credit's due, they motivate their staff to perform better. This also alleviates mediocrity and marginal production.

Monotonous Work:

When companies implement job rotation for their employees, they're attempting to make their employees' jobs more interesting. Job rotation involves several employees who work at substantially the same class or level of work and pay range. Employers who use job rotation reap extra benefits, because people can fill more than one job and are motivated to do a better job. Then, if employees are away sick, they're less likely to come back to work with a 'downer' when they're faced a mountain of work. If your company hasn't tried Job Rotation, suggest they try it!

Little Opportunity to Try New Ideas:

Another prime de-motivator occurs when supervisors refuse to listen to their staff when they try to explain better ways of doing their work. If supervisors can't implement their ideas, at least they should explain why they can't.

No New Skill Growth:

At one time, companies spent training dollars on their people and still couldn't keep up with the demand for competent qualified people. Recently companies have had to tighten their training budgets. Companies may refuse to give training that they believe employees can't use right away. Employees whose promotions are six months to one year away may find it difficult to obtain training.

Supervisors should encourage staff to obtain the training they need (on their own if necessary). The employee will reap benefits far beyond the costs they would invest in training. This gives the employee an edge over others who have not obtained this training on their own.

Poor fit between abilities and job requirements:

Before the economic downturn, many employees projected that they would climb the ladder in their companies very quickly. They now find they are over-qualified for their present positions. If the expected promotion is still far in the future, they may decide to move to another company.

Other staff members may be in the wrong kind of job, but don't know where to turn for help. These employees simply 'put in time' on the job. If a supervisor notices this behaviour they might be reluctant to suggest career counselling for them because they're afraid they might lose the employee. However, they'll likely lose them anyway and often career counselling can identify areas the staff member can move to in the future. They'll probably need to take night courses to prepare for their new career choice. In the meantime, they'll likely continue working for you while they're doing this. They'll be much more motivated to do a good job for you because of your caring attitude. You'll eventually lose them, but they'll be good workers in the meantime.

Common Ways We See Anger Expressed at Work:

1. Direct 'Take that':

When faced with a frustrating condition at work, many employees respond by directly attacking the condition. This may develop new procedures proving the theory that 'necessity is the mother of invention.' However if the frustrating condition continues we're likely to see direct expressions of hostility that are destructive in intent. Or we may see some of the less direct.

Example:

An employee may know a faster; better way of completing a task, but the supervisor won't let him/her do it his/her way. S/he can become disgruntled and his/her productivity level will suffer. S/he'll become a 'middle of the road' employees who appear to have tunnel vision.

2. Sabotage 'Let's get back at them':

Sabotage in the work place usually takes a much milder form than we typically associate with this word. Yet subtle forms of sabotage at work are very common. The work slow-down, the omitted procedure or the small error, are all evidence of the frustration-anger model at work.

Example: A personal assistant intentionally makes lousy coffee, because she feels it's not her responsibility. (This task should have been listed on her job description along with standards of performance on how the task should have been completed).

3. Over-compliance 'If that's what you want ...'

One excellent way of expressing anger at the frustrating boss is to do exactly what s/he asks regardless of the circumstances. The boss can't fault this practice, because after all, it's what s/he said. But s/he didn't mean to be taken so literally! When a union wants to make life difficult for management, members start going by the letter, rather than the spirit of the contract (work-to-rule).

Example:

You've given an employee a set of instructions on how to complete a project. You assume s/he will use his/her common sense and add pertinent information necessary to complete the assignment. S/he didn't - the report is useless.

4. Emotional withdrawal 'They aren't that important':

One way to deal with continuing frustration is to deny the importance of the blocking conditions. This is the familiar 'sour grapes' attitude. We often see employees become apathetic and just 'go through the motions' on the job (nine to fivers). Their actions say, this job isn't that important (just put in time). The really important things for them are outside the job (hate their jobs). If the interest and energy many workers spend on becoming star bowlers could be rekindled on the job, productivity gains would be considerable. Do this kind of employee a favour and encourage him/her to obtain career counselling to help him/her find out what s/he wants to do.

Example:

An employee follows her job description to a 'T.' you, as her supervisor, know she's capable of much more.

5. Turning inward 'It must be me':

One pathetic result of prolonged frustration is the tendency of some to turn their anger inward upon themselves. It can also happen when employees have written warnings on their file or have been demoted. Instead of venting their anger against the blocking conditions through direct or indirect means, the individual begins to attack him or herself. S/he winds up with a feeling of *'I'm no good.'* Turning such a person around is an immense supervisory challenge.

Example:

An employee who has taken a risk and has been 'burned' - may retreat into themselves and refuse to make decisions - use tunnel-vision in completing assignments - won't take risks - must feel safe in any decision they make.

The Right of appeal:

The 'Right of Appeal' is used by the supervisor and the employee only after they have made serious attempts to settle a dispute. The third person or mediator is usually the Human Resources Manager, union representative or any trained negotiator who can remain objective about the conflict.

Companies that don't offer the 'Right of Appeal' (which are usually non-union firms) are missing a very effective management tool.

Sometimes, in a non-union environment, when an employee and his/her supervisor disagree on an important issue, the employee simply gives up and leaves the company. The company may lose a valuable employee, but the situation was such that s/he felt s/he would never be able to solve the situation. This is why companies need to recognise that employees and supervisors alike require an impartial person to intervene and help them settle their disputes.

Supervisors and managers should remember:

a) They're not always right - appeal procedures protect staff from a supervisor's occasional lapses into biased opinion.
b) Ensure they listen effectively to their employees' reasoning behind their actions.
c) If they and their employee can't agree - they need to involve another impartial third party.
d) Both parties must be willing to change their mind and be open to suggestions and to welcome this appeal method as an aid rather than a threat.

CHAPTER SIX

TRAINING AND DEVELOPMENT

Qualities of a good trainer:

Trainers need many qualities to be successful. Some are used by those researching and preparing seminars. For instance:

1. Good research ability;
2. Attention to detail;
3. Ability to determine training needs;
4. Ability to prepare a seminar/workshop to meet those training needs;
5. Ability to sift through research material and take out only what is applicable;
6. Good knowledge of training methods;
7. Good sense of timing - able to time segments to keep learners interest;
8. Ability to prepare interesting sessions with variety and different methods of presenting material; and
9. Well organised.

Those who actually present seminars require the following qualities:

1. Interested in people;
2. Like dealing with people;
3. Knowledge of the subject being taught;
4. Good verbal and presentation skills;
5. Self-assured;
6. Well organised;
7. Empathetic to others;
8. Good listener;
9. Ability to 'bring out' quiet participants;
10. Ability to create an atmosphere of learning;
11. Does not threaten participants;
12. 'In tune' with the mood of the group;
13. Ability to read others' body language;
14. Ability to 'ad lib;'

15. Sense of humour;
16. Ability to explain information and skill knowledge in a clear, concise manner that is clearly understood by the participants;
17. Adaptable;
18. Perceptive;
19. Patient;
20. Radiates confidence;
21. Punctual, prepared and professional;
22. Good physical appearance; and
23. High energy level,

#21 is crucial to the success of a presenter. It's unforgivable for a trainer to be late for a session. If they're not properly prepared - all they do is waste everyone's time. If they don't conduct themselves professionally, they won't gain the respect of the audience, nullifying the content of the training session. Many adult learners would simply leave the session.

Teaching Adults:

As people grow older, it becomes more and more difficult to change established behaviour. Society has often encouraged people to be closed-minded towards new ideas. The creativity curve in most children levels off between six and eight years of age. This is when society dumps more negative criticism on children than positive. Therefore, when they become adults, they're often much more comfortable with negative criticism than with praise. They're used to feeling bad, rather than good about themselves.

If you've been trained as a teacher of children, you'll likely 'bomb' at teaching adults, because an entirely different approach is necessary. Adults feel that this type of instructor 'talks down to them.' Teachers would be more in tune and perceptive if they treated child learners in this manner as well. Children respond better if they're treated as if they are 'little adults.'

As trainers, your major responsibility may be to overcome the negative feelings your participants obtained in school as a child. This is accomplished by providing an atmosphere conducive to learning with low-risk factors for the individuals.

Many people resist taking responsibility for their actions and their own futures. The book 'The Cinderella Complex' by Collette Dowling describes this phenomenon in women. It explains how most women, live their lives under the assumption that someone else will look after them. Therefore, they have difficulty making any decision without getting the advice of at least one other person. They, in effect, resist taking responsibility for their actions and therefore their futures as well.

As a trainer, you'll need to overcome this obstacle. Men, too, may drift into this. They let the 'organisation or Big Brother' make all their work decisions for them - to determine their career paths. They float through life, making few direct decisions for themselves.

Our present social system heavily encourages dependence, conformity, submission and role-playing as the norm. Others follow their urges and grow, take risks, change and take charge of their lives and destiny. Sometimes, though, this growth and change can be painful.

For instance, a male employee attends a workshop on 'Interpersonal Skills' - returns to work but runs into difficulties. He's anxious to use his new skills, but finds his co-workers and supervisor are sceptical of his actions. Often he's forced to revert back to his old pattern (even if it was a bad one) so he doesn't 'make waves.' The training was useless!

Follow-up sessions would enable trainers to see whether participants were able to use the skills effectively in their work environment.

As instructors, you'll need to be in tune with the objectives of the group - be able to motivate them to learn the necessary information and new skills. It takes a particular kind of person to do this.

Giving training as a 'reward or a perk' for good performance or because George hasn't had any training this year; are poor reasons for sending anyone to training sessions. Training should be for specific reasons only.

Try to make sure attendees are there because they desire and need the training being offered. It's a good idea to determine the driving and restraining forces that might be in place for the trainees. One restraining force to learning might be a heavy workload that's piling up while they attend the training. Try to have someone take over their duties while they're away so they can concentrate on the training.

Determine at the beginning of the session why each of them feels the training session they're at will benefit them (learner's objectives). You might find out as I did that half the participants of an in-house training program were there under duress. Some may not have known they were to attend the seminar until the day before the session started.

If you have to face this kind of situation, say, *'I know some of you are here under duress and didn't ask for this training. I'd like you to decide whether you're going to put in time here at this session or are you going to 'fool them and learn something? What you will learn today can be used in all facets of your lives.'* I tried this and was surprised by the positive results. I had given the choice back to the participants. They now could choose what their attention level would be during the seminar. Most decided to 'fool them and learn something.'

Characteristics of adult learners:

There are certain characteristics that distinguish adult learners in general, from child learners.

1. Most adults are highly motivated to learn as long as it applies to their needs.
2. Adults like to take part in determining their own training needs.
3. Adults like sequential learning, with graduated stages of learning - lots of feedback and re-enforcement from their trainer.
4. Adults enjoy the novelty in learning - but can be 'turned off' or frightened by some ideas if they're too far out.
5. Adults have difficulty being re-trained; have set ideas on how to do things. Trainers need to show them why the new idea or method is superior to the old one.
6. An authoritarian set-up for learning is not acceptable and often increases the risk factor.
7. Learning will be retained if it's used as soon as possible.

114

8. Adults have set patterns of behaviour - this pattern has to be 'unset' in order for learning to take place.
9. Adults usually require a longer time to 'lock-in' and do tasks a different way.
10. Adults are less tolerant of 'busy work' which doesn't have immediate or direct application to their own objectives.
11. The older adult may have restricted powers of adjustment to external forces and distractions. They require more constant and ideal environmental conditions in order to learn or work efficiently.
12. Because adult learners are typically evening or 'after work' students, they're more likely to be physically and mentally tired. This makes them less alert when coming to class. This however, is offset by their increased desire to learn.
13. Adults have more experience in living, which gives them the advantage of being more readily able to relate new facts to experience.
14. Training is mainly a voluntary decision for them and their attendance often represents a considerable sacrifice. Having made this important and commendable decision, they expect (and deserve) the trainer's respect and to be treated as adult learners.

Differences in adult and child learners:

1. Adults are more realistic. They've lived longer and have a different perspective of life. They no longer see life through rose-colored glasses, but as a set of realities.
2. Adults have had more experience. They have insights and see relationships not discerned by children. They've accumulated wisdom that gives them a sense of what's likely to work and what's not.
3. Adults have needs that are more concrete and immediate than those of children. They're impatient with long discourses on theory and like to see theory applied with practical solutions.
4. Adults are not a captive audience. They attend voluntarily and if their interest is lacking, they're inclined to stop attending.
5. Adults expect to be treated as mature persons and resent having instructors talk down to them.

6. Adults enjoy having their talents, abilities and offered information made use of in a teaching situation.
7. Adult groups are likely to be more diversified than youth groups. Differences increase with age and mobility. Therefore, adult learners come from a wider variety of backgrounds.
8. Adults, through their fifties and beyond, can learn as well as youth. They may not perform some assignments as rapidly as children because of a slowing up of physical functions.
9. Adults attend classes often with a mixed set of motives - educational, social, recreational and sometimes out of a sense of duty.
10. Adults may be tired when attending classes. Some may have been working all day or attending to the needs of their families. They appreciate teaching devices that add interest and liveliness such as variety of methods, audio-visual aids, change of pace, short breaks or instructor with a sense of humour.

Learning process:

Learning involves personal change, which each trainee responds to differently. Motivation is the most important factor of learning. People learn what they want to learn, when they want to learn and under what conditions. Keeping up with or ahead of their peer group may be a motivator. It could simply be the need to learn, to keep advancing or to earn more money.

If the conditions of learning are not satisfactory, such as:

- Room too hot or too cold;
- Chairs uncomfortable;
- Too much distracting noise;
- Lights too bright (usually fluorescent);
- Not enough variety in learning;
- They're there under duress or pressed for time;
- They have a feeling of failure due to the atmosphere or the style of instruction.

They will likely feel that the training was a waste of their time.

The ability to learn has its limitations because of the person's motor skills or level of intellect. A trainee learns best by

116

participating in the learning process. The learner must be able to predict where they will use the learning. This is usually identified by the trainer supplying a list of training objectives for the session. The trainer would describe similarities in different ways until the learners recognise and understand the connection of the learning material to their personal situation.

How to 'lock-in' training:

Unless verbal data is repeated many times, it will be poorly retained. A combination of verbal and written material is far superior for retention of information by the trainee. Keep in mind that trainees retain:

- 10% of what they read (handouts, manuals).
- 20% of what they hear (have explained to them).
- 30% of what they see done (demonstrations).
- 40% of what they read and hear.
- 50% of what they read, hear and see demonstrated.
- 70% of what they read, hear, see done and they explain what they're going to do (a form of paraphrasing).
- 90% of what they read, hear, see done, they explain what they're going to do and then demonstrate themselves.

So trainers are encouraged to use all of the above to 'lock in' training. Most stop at the 50% mark. Encourage feedback from trainees to ensure that they did understand the teaching. It will also make them better listeners because there will be a 'test' (they will have to paraphrase what the trainer taught them).

Here's how to utilise the above information:

1. Trainer gives a handout that shows the steps participants will take to complete the task (10% retention).
2. Trainer explains the information on the handouts (20% retention).
3. Trainer demonstrates to the trainee how to complete the task (30% retention).
4. When both the handout is given and the trainer explains the information (40% retention).
5. When you use all three of the above (50% retention).

6. In addition to 4, ask the trainee to use paraphrasing to explain verbally what they're going to do (70% retention).
7. In addition to 4 and 5, trainee demonstrates for the trainer how s/he will complete the task.

This method uses the trainee's sight, hearing and touch senses. It encourages learners to be better listeners. Give learner written back-up information for future reference and have them use the training as soon as possible.

Recall is another training fundamental. Some may forget the overall training, but can recall something they've learned which stimulates more memory of the issues taught in the course. An atmosphere of approval and acceptance where participants can offer ideas and confirm their thought-patterns relating to the issues is essential for true learning.

Refresher training courses re-enforce the original information given, but are usually presented in a more capsulated form. One also tends to repeat behaviour that seems to bring rewards and not repeat behaviour that seems to be without reward or to bring punishment.

For example, a test is given and errors are corrected. Using positive feedback the trainer would say, *'You had the majority of it right. This is the only area where you went astray.'* Concentrate on what they did right, not what they did wrong!

One-on-one training:

1. Explain verbally how to do it.
2. Show them how to do it.
3. Have them explain to you, how they're going to do it.
4. Have them show you how they're going to do it.
5. Give them written back-up information.

Determining training needs:

Training needs must be established before writing or implementing any training program. This is normally the job of the researcher or the person preparing the training package or manual. You can determine training needs by or from:

- Performance appraisals. (Chapter 4 identifies how you would accomplish this.)
- Exit interviews - may identify that the employee left because the company didn't meet his/her training needs.
- Supervisors identify performance problems.
- Clients - usually in the form of complaints.
- Organisational requirements - new equipment, policies, procedures or new ways of doing things company-wide.
- Union requirements.
- Technological advances - to upgrade employee's knowledge - usually an ongoing occurrence in most companies.
- Recruiters - the gap between qualification of candidates and the requirements of the position.
- Employees themselves ask for training.
- Production / work output - problems or new methods determined.
- Morale problems.
- Company questionnaires.
- Accident statistics.

You may have identified the following that have training needs:

- Individuals for personal upgrading;
- Group needs (learning how to use a new computer); or
- Organisation-wide training (implementation of a new performance appraisal system).

To determine individual needs for training, a company may administer the following tests:

Testing abilities of employees:

The following are more objective tests:

a) **General intellectual abilities**: These are not typical I.Q. tests, but are more job-related and determine verbal comprehension and reasoning abilities.
b) **Interests and motivation tests:** Are difficult tests to assess because people tend to give answers they think are expected of them. To obtain correct assessment, questions

must be skilfully worded. The person evaluating these tests requires considerable training themselves.

c) **Aptitude tests**: Determine a person's capacity to obtain new levels of knowledge, skills and attitudes from training.

d) **Achievement tests**: Measures what an employee knows, understands or can do in relation to specific areas of knowledge or skill.

e) **Motor skill tests:** Involve physical agility, manual dexterity and sense of hearing, vision and touch. These are used where motor abilities are essential for successful completion of duties of a position.

f) **Interpersonal and leadership skills**: Assessed from work history and references from present and former supervisors.

g) **Personal history data**: Begins with the application form or resume and information from an employee's personnel file. This information includes previous education, experience, credentials, membership and occasionally reference checks.

h) **Current performance and potential:** Assessed by performance appraisals and employee's capability for learning.

Dimensions tested:

These are more subjective and only used in conjunction with objective information gathered. They are valuable for determining training needs in areas that are not as tangible to evaluate as objective ones:

1. **Speaking ability**: Ability to effectively express oneself in both individual and group situations.
2. **Listening ability:** Ability to pick out important information in oral communication.
3. **Writing ability:** Ability to express ideas in a clear, concise, grammatically correct manner.
4. **Reading ability:** Ability to obtain facts and comprehend meaning in written communication.
5. **Ability to analyse:** Ability to identify and interpret the key elements of a situation, concept or problem.
6. **Judgement:** Ability to evaluate situations and/or information and reach logical conclusions.

7. **Decisiveness:** Readiness to make decisions on the basis of sound judgment.
8. **Plan and organise:** Ability to effectively plan and organise their own work and direct or assist others in planning and organising their work.
9. **Delegate:** Ability to delegate tasks in a manner conducive to effectiveness and subordinate development.
10. **Control:** Ability to effectively use administrative controls for evaluation, auditing and monitoring functions.
11. **Leadership:** Ability to guide a group or individual to where they can effectively accomplish a task.
12. **Flexibility:** Ability to modify their approach and/or behaviour as required.
13. **Empathy:** Awareness, understanding and consideration of the needs and feelings of others.
14. **Initiative:** Ability to motivate themselves to take positive action and have a 'sense of urgency.'
15. **Tolerance** to stress: Ability to maintain expected performance levels under stress.
16. **Co-operative philosophy:** Ability to perceive and show positive reaction to current needs and future expectations of the company.
17. **Creativeness:** Ability to generate imaginative solutions to problem situations.

Manpower planning:

When determining training needs it's important to evaluate the present situation. Companies use manpower planning to compare the demands of the corporation vs. the supply of manpower to define immediate needs and establishes long-range requirements.

Demand:
Refers to the perceived demands of an organisation determined by budgetary requests, predicted expansions, changes in technology (usually determined in five year forecasts).

Supply:
The existing supply of manpower less turnover, retirement, attrition, etc. Often companies have senior people who are ready to retire. They suddenly realise there's no one to replace them or they realise there'll be a gap if they promote someone to a higher

level. Manpower planning keeps this from happening and uses and expands the skills of existing employees.

Every department needs to produce a Job Skills Inventory Chart that determines whether they have enough back-up staff to fill in for staff members that are away for holidays or because of illness. They make a chart of every task that needs to be completed in the department and determines who is qualified to cover those tasks. You may be surprised to learn that some of your employees are not 'duplicated.' If they're away, your department could come to a grinding halt, so it's a worthwhile endeavour to recommend for every department.

Training needs of supervisors:

The supervisor who finds that s/he is constantly describing his/her staff as 'second rate,' is in essence, describing his/her own performance. This supervisor's not providing the proper training guidelines and motivation for co-operation of his/her employees. Many of these supervisors haven't had the basic training required to do their job properly. Or it's possible their managers didn't have the basic training required to get the job done either so are poor role models.

Supervisors have the responsibility of not only delegating work, checking work, etc., but to:

- Identify training needs;
- Provide on-the-job training;
- Help develop training programs; and
- Take part in training to meet the needs of any new policy or technology that affects his/her staff.

It's not enough to provide the above to employees. The employees, themselves must:

Be willing to perform:
Resistance can be cultural, personal, an unwillingness to take risks; work environment may not be conducive (kind of supervision etc.) types of employees, general work attitudes. The supervisor's attitude controls seventy-five percent of this area.

Have the ability to perform:
Correct this by offering proper training.

Have the Opportunity:
Could be self-generated (employee asks for the opportunity) or their supervisor offers it for developmental purposes or through necessity to stay on the job.

Learning a new skill:

Teaching someone a new skill takes talent and perseverance. Use of paraphrasing helps implant information. As learners, we all pass through four definite stages when learning something new. These stages are:

Unconscious Incompetence
They aren't even aware that they lack the skill. For example - they may not even have known that the skill of Paraphrasing existed.

Conscious Incompetence
They're aware that they lack the skill. For example, before they learned how to drive a car, they knew they couldn't drive a car.

Conscious Competence
They know the techniques of the skill but have to stop and think before they reacted. *'Do I push the clutch in first or do I turn on the key first?'*

Unconscious Competence
The skill is now well established and automatic. They probably don't even think about what they're doing when they drive - they're on 'automatic pilot.'

It takes six weeks to 'lock into' how to do something new and up to three months to 'lock-into' doing something differently than how they did it before.

Retention of information:

Those who are responsible for training have probably thrown their hands in the air at times. Their information seems to go in one ear and out the other with some learners. Many people require constant repetition of instructions. This type of person is probably a poor listener.

Information has a better chance of being 'locked in' when trainers use a variety of training methods. This could be with visual aids such as movies, slides or flip charts. To further 'lock in' the training, see that they use the training as soon as possible.

Training of others:

If you've had the responsibility of training others, you've probably had to explain how to do something more than once. Paraphrasing is a very effective tool to use when training others, especially if they're lazy listeners. To help them retain their training, do the following:

1. Give them short, sequential instructions.
2. State, *'To make sure that I was clear in my instructions to you, could you please explain what you're going to do?'*
3. If they give you a blank look and are unable to relate the steps.
4. Repeat the short, sequential instructions.
5. Again ask them to relate the steps they will take to complete the task.

You'll find that their listening skills will improve immeasurably. They'll know that when you train them to do anything new, there will be a *test* to see if they've listened properly. You'll find that instruction-giving will be much easier for you in the future.

Do however remember that the onus is on you to make your instructions clear. Using such questions as:

'Do you understand?' (This doesn't confirm that they did understand what you asked them to do).

'Explain what I want you to do.' (This will just get their backs up).

'Did you catch that?' (This is a put-down, because you're insinuating that they aren't bright enough to pick up the information).

If they misunderstand you, it's much better to make the problem yours. You can accomplish this by statements such as:

'So I'm sure I was clear in my instructions to you ...'

'Let's see if I've been clear in my instructions to you.'

Then ask if they have any questions to clarify the training.

Training vs. development:

Training Need:

Exists any time employees require updating of existing skills or need to learn new ones.

Developmental Need:

Development deals with the full utilisation of the skills of every employee. It uses the abilities learned during training or uses the innate skills of each employee. It's excellent for motivating employees to do their very best and can assist them to reach the 'self actualisation' level in motivation.

Development:

When you think of the development of people, what do you usually think of? Most people probably would identify formal training. If employees require development, we think of sending them off somewhere else to attend classes, courses, conferences, workshops and seminars. The most significant development of a person takes place on-the-job. 87 per cent of a person's development takes place on the job and the person's boss is the most important teacher in his/her work life.

Compare development to an elastic band. It expands the knowledge learned in training. Unless a person expands his/her horizons, s/he won't be able to stretch when necessary. Developmental opportunities come up during a normal day, but we often don't think of them as developmental. Let's see if you can identify development vs. training. Assume that your boss said the following things to you. Which statements do you see as developmental and which as training?

Decide for each question:

TNG for Training   **DEV for Development**

1. What would you recommend?
2. I'm going to show you how our new computer system works. You'll be using it from now on.
3. I'm not going to make your decisions for you, but I'll certainly discuss your problem with you whenever you wish.

4. Tell me only what you feel I should know about your operations and why you feel I should be aware of these things.
5. Please attend this planning meeting in my place. You know our goals and have full authority to commit us to whatever course of action you feel is appropriate.
6. I'd like you to attend the meeting on safety that all the employees are attending.
7. You didn't make the decision to cancel the project soon enough. Let's review it together, to see what we should have done to reduce our losses.
8. Here's a special project for you that will give you experience in a new area. When you finish a plan for accomplishing it, bring it in and show me what you suggest to do.
9. The head of our treasury group mentioned the fine co-operation he has been getting from you. Keep up the good work.
10. Here's a book on management that I just read. When you've had a chance to read it, let's get together and discuss it. We may find ways of improving our operations.

Only numbers 2 and 6 involved training - the rest are developmental. How did you do?

Career development:

On-the-job career development occurs under these conditions:

- Job rotation;
- Special tasks;
- Acting capacity for more senior position;
- Asked for advice;
- Team effort;
- Allowed to make decisions;
- Problem-solving;
- New duties; or
- Assist supervisor with tasks.

Setting up a Training Plan

Whenever you need to research, prepare and present a training session, follow this procedure to set up a training plan to meet your training needs:

126

1. **List problems**. Most training requirements surface when problems occur. Examine these problems to see if they are the real problems.

2. **Determine training needs** to delete problems. Here are some Sample Training Needs:

   - Problem-solving capability of several employees requires improvement.
   - Employees must learn how to handle change or new situations.
   - Communication skills require improvement.
   - Work ethic and attitude to work need to change.
   - Establish orientation program to help employees understand the organisation better.
   - Employees must learn how to use our new computer.
   - Supervisors need to learn how to delegate and motivate their subordinates better.
   - Time management problems due to overdue reports and work overloads.
   - Third shift being put into place - train full crew in the use of the equipment.

3. **Set training objectives to meet training need.** These objectives must be realistic and within the scope of learning of the group or person being trained. The objectives must be specific (tangible - easy to measure) rather than general (intangible - difficult to measure) i.e.:

   General Objective: Improve interpersonal skills of employee
   Specific Objective: List 8 steps in the communication process.
   Objectives require three pieces of information to be valid (quality, quantity and time). When setting objectives, ask yourself - what is it I want the learner to be able to do after training?

   After setting the objectives, determine the conditions under which you expect the result to occur: i.e.

   - given a list of ...
   - without the aid of notes ...

- on the job ...
- or whatever help you provide or deny the participant: i.e. After five hours of dual flight time, following all safety and flight rules, the student will be able to land the airplane safely without help from the instructor.

Conditions: After 5 hours of dual flight time, following all safety and flight rules and without help from the instructor, participant will be able to ...

Minimal level of achievement: Will be able to land the airplane safety without help from the instructor.

4. **Write training program**. Consider the following when writing a training program:

   a) **Participants:** Size of group, familiarity with subject and their sex (females participate in class participation portions more than males) age, ethnic makeup, belief systems, voluntary/mandatory attendance.
   b) **Fun:** Be creative, exciting, vs. all assignments and work.
   c) **Time:** Task time, reflection time, breaks.
   d) **Appropriate sequencing**:
      Introduction - get their attention, introduce yourself (if time and appropriate, have them introduce themselves). Explain format and obtain interest/excitement.
      Body - Present concepts, skills, awareness.
      Conclusion - What they've learned, what they can use tomorrow, what they can use later, how to retain the information, etc.
   (e) **Skill Complexity:** Easy? Difficult? In-between?
   (f) **Risk factor to participants:** Light? Heavy?
   (g) **Practice:** Instructor demonstration / Class participation.
   (h) **Atmosphere conducive to learning**: Comfortable surroundings, attitude of the instructor etc.
   (i) **Variety:** Lecture, films, PowerPoint presentations, overheads. length of segments, media used (activity).
   (j) **Method of Instruction:** (covered later).
   (k) **Intensity of Training:** High? Low?
   (l) **Costs:**

5. Evaluate and validate training.

> **Evaluation:** Relates to the methods used in learning during the training. Determine this with the use of tests and follow-up to see if trainees have learned what was taught. This can be done at the end of training or as late as a year later. This is done in class or on-the-job and will use several measuring devices (how it affected the people involved etc.)

> **Validation of Training:** Relates to the course content of the training session. Was it geared towards reaching the learning objectives? If not – the training wasn't valid and was a waste of training time and effort.

6. Tangible/intangible behaviour:

> When identifying objectives of training, use only tangible behaviours:

> **Tangible**: Measurable and objective such as:
> At the end of training, participants will be able to:
> Write; recite; identify; differentiate; find; solve; construct; demonstrate; express; state; choose; explain; give; define; relate; determine; describe; or present.

> **Intangible**: Hard to measure and subjective such as:
> At the end of the training, participants will be able to:
> Understand; remember; recognise; be aware of; perceive; appreciate; have knowledge of; know; comprehend; familiar with; realise; or acquainted with.
> You will see that these would be difficult to measure. Use only tangible and measurable words when setting objectives.

Setting objectives:

To put the training picture in perspective, you will determine the following:

Tangible behaviour: Using action words, which describe something you can observe them, doing.
Conditions: Explains your method of training and when you expect training to be effective.
Minimal Level of Achievement:
Usually quantity, quality and time.

Here are sample objectives from my Train the trainer seminar:

Objectives of Learning:

General: Participants will learn how to prepare and present training programs to meet specific training needs of adult learners.

Specific Conditions: At the end of the seminar, by examining presented information, through discussion, group activities, self study, assignments, training films and practice lecture,

Level of Achievement: participants should be able to: (Tangible behaviour)

- Describe 19 qualities of a good training facilitator
- Relate 14 characteristics of adult learners
- Identify learner's needs through 13 training assessment methods
- Show 13 methods of instruction
- Explain the meaning of the terms Training and Development and give an example of each
- Write 5 ingredients for setting training objectives
- Define tangible and intangible behaviour and give an example of each
- Express the meaning of Theoretical and Practical training and where each is used.
- Give the differences between Technical and Personal Growth training and give an example of each
- State the uses of 5 different training aids
- Recite 5 steps in the Training Procedure
- Demonstrate 2 kinds of training re- enforcement and give an example of each
- List 6 steps used in one-on-one training that are most effective for retention of information
- Differentiate the 8 steps in the communication process
- Define Paraphrasing and give one example of how it can be used in training
- Relate normal speaking and listening speeds
- Choose 2 methods of keeping participants motivated to learn
- Present 2 tips relating to what instructors should wear when training

Identifying costs of training:

You'll need to establish training costs to establish a budget. These expenses could be:

1. Room rental;
2. Equipment rental – PowerPoint projector; video recorder and monitor; overhead projector and screen; slide projector; flip chart, blackboard or whiteboard; podium or a microphone;
3. Handouts and overheads;
4. Refreshments and meals;
5. Advertising, brochures, memos, etc. (if necessary).
6. Notepaper, pens, pencils, binders, name tags, etc.; Cost of instructor / resource people - their fee, travelling expenses etc.; and
7. Man-hours of employees who are away from productive work and an estimate of time loss and cost of employees not doing their duties while at the training session;

Methods of Instruction:

There are many ways to train participants:

Seminars/Workshops:
You can accomplish a lot by these one or two day sessions. This rapid orientation is especially effective with an audience that's alert, interested and anxious to learn.

Lecture method:
On the surface, it's one of the most efficient methods for imparting ideas. A lecturer in one hour can cover a large number of ideas and/or areas of instruction. Speed of coverage and efficiency is the advantage of the lecture method. Its disadvantage is that much of the lecturer's input can be lost because nothing in the participant's own experience might relate to the information. It's best used in combination with other methods.

Theory/Practical/Example/Lecture:
This is where a trainer explains a complicated theory and gives a practical application of the theory. The trainer then asks participants to give an example of how they could use the theory.

Case Studies:

Providing cases for participants to study and discuss has become a standard method. The advantage is strong involvement of participants and their own reactions. A disadvantage is the time consumed in writing a good case and in encouraging free and full participation and discussion.

Simulation:

Includes such techniques as role-playing, business and other games (computerised or manual). It has the same advantages/disadvantages mentioned for case discussions.

Multi-Media:

Many trainers use this method. It uses role-plays, films, cases, lectures etc. and has the multi-media approach. The general idea is to bombard every sense and 'ram' the message home to the participant. (This is my favourite).

Programmed Learning:

These are 'pre-packaged learning systems.' The major drawbacks are that they're normally very expensive and become obsolete very quickly. A secondary problem is that the facilitator did not prepare the program and may not have enough knowledge to answer participant questions about the content.

Correspondence and Home Study:

This method is inexpensive, convenient and can accomplish much. Its weakness is that it lacks immediate feedback and face-to-face contact. Learners require a high level of self-discipline.

Reading:

Many training personnel insist that reading changes nothing. Many participants are as adamant that a good book or a good idea in a book has 'changed their life.' It does give a good basis if used as a pre-requisite to attending a seminar or as back-up for future use after a seminar.

Laboratory Training:

This learning method helps participants analyse their own experiences and identifies other ways they could have handled situations better. Everyone in the group is encouraged to give their input.

Sensitivity Training:
Teaches participants how their behaviour affects others and how they can adapt their present behaviour to be more acceptable to others. (My Dealing with Difficult People uses this as part of the training package).

Encounter Training:
This is an adaptation of sensitivity training. It focuses on body movement, body touch and 'internal feelings.' Its major emphasis would seem to be on heightened awareness and enjoyment of feelings and emotions. This method may be very threatening to some participants.

Situational Training:
This method usually begins with some formal program of training. The participants are in 'family groups' that work and relate together on the job. Usually an outside trainer helps them to begin the process. The 'work group leader' takes on more and more of the training responsibility and uses on-going organisational problems as the learning vehicles.

It is a learn-as-you-do process and one of the sought-after benefits is to learn how to handle similar future problems. This is also the case when a supervisor involves his/her staff in brainstorming to come up with the best solutions to problems

Methods I use:

The method I use most often is the multi-media method, especially for one to three day seminars where people are in one place all the time. For active people, putting them in this kind of environment is not only uncomfortable, but not conducive to learning. Therefore, I must provide variety and movement of the participants to meet this need.

I use lecture, films, PowerPoint, handouts, questionnaires, role-plays, case studies, group and individual activities and discussion periods.

Preparing for a seminar / workshop:

Before presenting a seminar, do the following:

- Determine the training needs.
- Research the topic thoroughly.
- Make a list of objectives that will meet the training needs using tangible objectives.
- Choose from your research the material what you wish to use.
- Put into a semblance of order (a) (b) (c) so ideas flow. Provide comments that will bridge between similar areas of study.
- Brainstorm to determine the best method of presenting the information to the group (through lecture, handouts, films, discussions etc.)
- Choose which training aids you'll use. Be sure to preview films and that PowerPoint and overhead projectors, video cassettes, slide projector, etc. are all in working order.
- Work out timing for each segment - keeping in mind coffee and lunch breaks.
- (Remember the need for participants to move around occasionally).
- Prepare a leader's guide.
- Prepare handouts, PowerPoint Presentations, slides and overheads.
- Revise program as necessary.
- Choose class size and room set-up best suited to the program.
- Determine risk level for participants (group activities are less risky for participants - don't make risks too high at the beginning of the seminar).
- Set the date for training (be careful choosing day of the week. Mid-week seems to suit most people).
- Have paper, pencils and folders or binders available for participants (optional).
- Be at training area at least one-half hour before class starts. Make sure all equipment, handouts, films etc. are there and in proper working order.
- Conduct training session.
- Evaluate and validate training.

Group vs. individual activities:

The risk factor to each individual increases when they have to speak in a classroom situation. Many participants will resist having to speak up in class to relate their experiences or ideas. Others may try to take over the class because they're too expressive in their comments and may dominate the group.

To bring out the quiet ones (using their name-tags to identify them) call them by name and ask them for their opinion on the topic. Have different people be spokespersons in group activities.

To quiet down the loud ones - state, *'The class is making John do too much work. It's time to give him a break and for the rest of you to speak up.'* In group participation sessions, encourage each participant to express his or her ideas - not just one person. Encourage different people to lead groups (especially the quiet ones).

A facilitator of a seminar must provide a climate of mutual trust, respect and openness, focusing on the positives in themselves and others. In group activities, participants are encouraged to share their problems and fears. There they can gain from the knowledge and resources of others who have been in similar situations and faced similar problems.

Group activities decrease the personal risk factor for learners. It gives several important advantages over one-to-one or individual experiences. Participants find comfort in knowing others share similar difficulties. It's often heard *'I thought I was the only one with that problem!'*

When you divide participants into groups, have them appoint a spokesperson before discussing the topic. Each subsequent group activity has a new spokesperson. As the spokesperson is speaking for the group (not themselves) even the quieter ones will feel less threatened.

In situations where you're pushing for assertiveness in public speaking, have the spokesperson make his/her presentation at the front of the class. Occasionally provide a microphone to increase learning of this new skill.

Technical vs. life skills:

Technical Training:
Use variety in training to keep the interest of participants at technical training sessions. Technical skills range from how to fix your car to how to run your computer. Technical skill training usually involves more homework and more concentration on the

part of the trainee. Many participants anticipate (and rightly so) there will be a test after the training. Therefore, the element of risk on the participant is higher. Examples of technical training given in the workplace are:

- Supervisory skills of any kind;
- Computer training;
- Product knowledge;
- Selling techniques;
- Problem solving and decision making;
- Employee discipline; and
- Employment interviewing.

Life Skill Training:
These are sessions that help a person grow in other than technical areas. Participants are likely to be more responsive and less threatened at life skills sessions. Examples of Life Skill training are:

- Interpersonal skills;
- Stress management;
- Time management;
- Assertiveness training; and
- Non-verbal communication.

Practical vs. Theoretical vs. training:

Practical:
Designed to supplement theoretical training by experience actively engaged in some course of action

I use a mixture of the above methods. For example:

a) I introduce a theory i.e. Maslow's Hierarchy of Needs.

b) I give practical examples of the theory. i.e.: When training participants; it's an asset to know where they fit - what motivates them to learn. Is it a need:

    (i)   to obtain information to fulfil the obligations of their position which would allow them to put bread on the table (Physiological need) or,

    (ii)   is their job in jeopardy because, if they don't learn the information, they may lose their job (security need) or,

136

    (iii)   will they remain behind their peers if they don't obtain the needed information (social needs) or,

    (iv)   they may not obtain a promotion depending on whether they learn the information (ego needs).

  c) Have participants decide how this theory and practical application apply to their own specific situation or needs. They're encouraged to give examples of where and when they would use it.

Theoretical:

- The analysis of a set of facts in their relation to one another
- A plausible or scientifically acceptable general principle offered to explain the phenomena

Use of training aids:

Training aids are anything that you use to help your participants learn. For example:

- Name tags for tables;
- PowerPoint projector and computer;
- Audio-visual equipment;
- Video cassettes, CDs or DVDs;
- Overhead projector and transparencies;
- Slide projector;
- Flip charts, either prepared or blank with felt pens;
- Handouts/binders. Decide whether you'll give the handouts one at a time, all at once or in packages;
- Blackboard or whiteboard plus chalk and felt pens;
- Samples of forms or products;
- Gimmicks (to lock-in training); and/or
- Guest speakers / resource people.

Timing of training segments:

I've found that this is a trial and error area. You'll have to anticipate how much time to leave for class participation. This, by the way, is the most unpredictable area of instructing. If you have a quiet group, you may find your timing is all off. If you have a group who really get into the discussion or (Heaven forbid) get a 'loudmouth,' you may find yourself running behind.

The first time I present a training program, I put estimated times in the margin of my leader's guide (in pencil). For instance - I'll write in the margin that a segment will run from 10:45 to 11:00 am. As I go through the first run-through, I write, 'needs more time' or 'took less time' which I implement for the next session. Soon I have a good idea of how much time I really need. The more proficient you become at presenting seminars, the better you'll become in this area.

Bridging:

Try to have one topic flow into another by bridging two topics. For example: If I was talking about the different methods of training I could use, I might bridge onto the topic of costs. I'd say, *'One thing to consider along with what method you choose is the cost of each method of training.'* Then I'd bridge into explaining the importance of proper timing of training programs, etc.

Re-enforcement of training:

Participants want to know ahead of time what's being taught. Being able to measure personal progress increases the participant's motivation to learn and retain the training. They must use the training to retain it. Teaching an employee a new skill they won't use right away is a waste of training.

For example: Teaching an employee supervisory skills, when it's known that it may be a year until they're able to use the skills. In some cases they're taught proper supervisory skills, but go back to an environment where their managers haven't had basic supervisory training. These managers balk at the 'new ideas' their supervisors give them on how they should be doing things.

Make sure that the manager and supervisor receive the same kind of training if you perceive this training is lacking in the manager. Suggest that the managers 'sit in' on the training session 'so they can monitor how well the supervisors do when they return to work.' This saves face for the manager and results in their receiving the necessary training.

How to keep participants motivated:

If your program has followed the suggestions I've made, you'll find that participants will stay motivated to learn. Watch your audience to see if you're losing them. Look for signs of restlessness, loss of eye contact, fewer questions, yawning. You can get them back by having them move around, give a stretch break, use a little humour. Try telling them they'll be having a test or give a change of pace.

Instructor's apparel:

Trainers should wear comfortable clothing and shoes suitable to the group being trained. Female trainers should not wear bold prints or stripes that are hard to watch for any length of time. Make sure your shoes are 'worn in.'

Presentation skills:

1. Are you projecting your voice properly? Should you be using a microphone for large groups? If so, what kind – on a podium, portable or clip-on? (Check for squeal or feedback).
2. When speaking in front of groups, exaggerate your gestures.
3. If you walk while you speak - don't pace or turn your back to your audience.
4. Don't talk when showing overheads, if participants are taking notes from the overhead or power point presentation.
5. Watch for your nervous habits while presenting such as clicking a pen; hand in and out of jacket pocket; smoothing or stroking hair etc.)
6. Use notes - don't rely on memory. You don't have to use them, but have them ready in case you lose your train of thought.
7. Use humour occasionally to keep participants interested.
8. Don't ramble on - be specific.
9. Dress one level above your audience.
10. Watch your audience for attention level and understanding of what you're explaining.
11. Make eye contact occasionally with members of your audience (short time only - 3 seconds maximum direct eye contact).
12. Don't use big words and use technical terms only when necessary.
13. When writing on a whiteboard or flip chart - don't stand in front of it; stand to the side, so they can see what you're writing. Don't have your back to them - stand to the side.
14. Keep extra strips of masking tape handy. Use these for a multitude of reasons.

15. A podium helps keep your notes out of sight. Don't however; spend all your time behind a podium unless you are delivering a speech using a fixed microphone. Use a mobile microphone if possible.
16. Have paper and pencil handy to jot down notes for follow-up especially after group discussions.
17. Have a wrap-up at the end of the seminar to review content of the seminar. Explain to participants that the training is only effective if it's used. Encourage them to follow-up on any areas identified during the session where they need improvement.

I ask three questions at the end of the seminar. The participants answer them and pass them in (anonymous information). These three questions are:

1. *'How well did this seminar meet your particular needs?'*
2. *'How could I improve this seminar for the next group?'*
3. *'What is the most significant thing you learned today?'*

Or sometimes I just ask #3 at the end of the session.

Training Agreements

Many companies have employees sign Employee Training Agreements. These agreements spell out the employee's responsibility to remain with the company for a set length of time when the company spends money on training on their behalf. For instance before they are sent to training courses, the cost of that training is identified. If the employee leaves the company before they have been there for two years, they give the company the right to dock their final pay with a percentage of what they would owe for the training received.

For instance: If the three-day training course cost the company $1,000 and the employee left after one year – the employee would have to pay back $500 of that training fee. If they only stayed six months, they would pay back $750 – eighteen months - $250.

Now that you're aware of how to deal with the training aspect of your job – we'll head onto the hardest part – that of disciplining and firing employees.

CHAPTER SEVEN

COUNSELLING INTERVIEWS

Why supervisors/managers hate disciplining their staff:

****

This section is information you can give to supervisors regarding their responsibilities as a supervisor. I use the word supervisor, but anyone who supervises others including managers, department heads, superintendants, CEOs and even presidents of companies need this information. They, not their Manager or a Human Resources specialist, are responsible for disciplining the people that report directly to them (except in the case of terminating an employee – then the Human Resources department would get involved).

Help them learn how to discipline their staff by passing on the information in this chapter and the following chapters.

****

When asked, *'What is their most distasteful task as a supervisor,'* disciplining their staff is always high on the list. They use such excuses as:

> *'I hate bawling anyone out.'*
> *'Maybe the situation isn't so bad anyway.'*
> *'Hopefully their behaviour will improve without my causing a fuss.'*

None of these excuses work. You may ask, *'I know I have to do and say something, but I don't know where to start. How can I get the results I want and make the experience easier for myself and fair to the employee I have to reprimand.'*

Have a meeting with the offending employee remembering that your main goal is to improve the conduct of the employee, not to make them want to retaliate or have hurt feelings over the interview. Remind yourself that one of your major supervisory functions is to check or 'critique' the work of those who work for you. This is different from criticising them. You'd be identifying the things they did right along with the things they did wrong. Your job is to get their best performance. To achieve this high

141

standard of performance you must evaluate the work they've completed.

You may be tempted to let things slide, but in the future they'll continue doing the task the 'wrong' way, if you don't catch them the first time they do something wrong. If you let it slide, the pattern may be locked in, which will be more difficult for the employee to change.

When critiquing work, give a summary of how they completed the task. In all likelihood, 98 per cent of the job was done correctly, so give a summary by saying something like, *'I'm very pleased with the results of this report. The only tiny correction I'd want made is that ... otherwise the rest of your performance was fine. I was impressed with the way you expressed yourself regarding the ... Keep up the good work!'*

Whenever you have to correct behaviour - don't say, *'You made a mistake.'* Instead say, *'In the future, I'd like you to complete this assignment this way.'* If you use this form of criticism, it will seldom be necessary to discipline an employee.

When an employee must be reprimanded for continued bad performance or behaviour, keep them informed at every stage, by explaining what the consequences will be if their undesirable behaviour or performance continues. Then it's the employee who chooses to misbehave, therefore they're the ones who initiate the discipline - not the supervisor or manager. When you've conducted yourself properly, you'll be able to get rid of the guilt feelings you may have, because you've had to reprimand an employee. When disciplinary meetings are carried out correctly, it's the employee who carries the burden of guilt, not the supervisor.

Some employees seem to have an excuse for everything they've done wrong and if you checked things out, you'd find they were telling the truth. But there are so many errors made! The employee's late for work, with reports and you're finding that things are rapidly getting out of hand. How should you deal with this? Keep reminding the employee that it's the results you're interested in, not his or her excuses. When delegating assignments, give deadlines and encourage the employee to meet those deadlines.

142

Supervisors must get work done through other people by planning organising, staffing, directing and controlling. As a supervisor, anything you delegate to others reflects on you. If you delegate a task to Sally and she doesn't do a good job - who's to blame? Sally? No, you are! Your employees either make you look good - or make you look bad, depending on how well they do the tasks you've assigned to them. You can't pass the buck to them by saying, *'I asked Sally to do it - I guess she didn't do it right.'* That's not good enough. You're still ultimately responsible for her actions as well as your own. So, if Sally doesn't do her job properly, you must talk to her and make attempts to improve her performance.

Firing probationary employees

Probationary employees are normally excluded from the coverage of the federal termination of employment laws. The probationary period must be determined upon hiring and if it is longer than three months, that it is reasonable because of the circumstances.

Probationary periods are viewed as similar to a fixed term contract, so that the contract of employment comes to an end and provided the employee is found to be satisfactory, a new contract of employment is entered into. Thus an employer is able to dismiss an employee (i.e.: refuse to offer further employment) at the end of a probationary period, without the employee having any legal redress. Notice should be given so that it expires before the end of the probationary period.

Probationary employees can also be dismissed prior to the expiry of the probationary period unless there is a contractual term or understanding between the parties (i.e.: an oral term in a contract of employment) to the contrary.

Make sure you look carefully at the new employee's behaviour and productivity before his/her probationary period is over. Two weeks before the probationary period is over, review the new employee's abilities. If there are any problems, call a meeting and explain his/her performance problems. If you're not yet sure, let the employee know that his/her probationary period is being extended (usually two to four more weeks).

Some employees simply don't fit in and the supervisor is faced with letting them go. Many don't know if there's a difference from a legal point of view between dismissing a probationary employee and dismissing a permanent one. The main difference between a probationary and a permanent one is that the employer has much more discretion to terminate the probationary employee. Until about ten years ago, the probationary employee had no protection. The employer had the right to terminate with no notice and didn't have to give reasons for dismissal. Nor did they give the employee an opportunity of changing his/her behaviour.

Now, the law is changed in favour of the employee. Although the probationary employee still has less job security, the employer must determine carefully whether the employee is suitable for the job and must give the employee the opportunity to correct his/her behaviour or performance discrepancies *before* the end of their probationary period. This is why you need to constantly check their work and behaviour during the probationary period. Waiting until the probationary period is up - is too late.

Disciplining former peers:

It's particularly difficult if the people you're now supervising are your former peers. What kind of problems could occur if you were chosen as the new supervisor of several of your former workmates?

- They may be jealous, envious or angry;
- Former peers may indulge in sabotaging efforts, gang up on you or become un-cooperative;
- They know your weaknesses and may take advantages of you;
- They may expect favouritism from you if you're a friend or expect you to show bias towards them if they know you don't like them;
- Will not show respect to you as their supervisor;
- May alienate themselves from you;
- May feel they're better qualified than you;
- *You* may go on a power or ego trip and mismanage your responsibilities

Because Human Resources was likely involved in this promotion, it's important that you ensure that the following happens:

1. The manager, who was responsible for giving the new supervisor the promotion, should explain to the unsuccessful candidates why they weren't chosen for the position.
2. On the first day the supervisor takes the position, the person they report to should call a meeting with the new supervisor and his/her staff. The manager introduces the new supervisor to the staff, making a statement such as, *'I expect all of you to give the same performance for our new supervisor as you did for Bill Jones who's now been promoted to another position.'* The manager then leaves the room and hands over the meeting to the new supervisor.

Have a talk with the new supervisor, before the day s/he starts the position. Here's the advice you should give to him/her:

How you continue with the meeting from this point onward is crucial to how you're ultimately accepted in the position. What would you do? Would you go over what changes you wished to make? Explain that you'll do your best to fill the position? How would you start out?

If you don't deal with the negative feelings that are there, you're lost from day one and will probably have to put up with many negative actions from your former peers. Instead, deal with the major problem by saying, *'I know several of you applied for this position and I can understand if you're disappointed because you weren't chosen for this position. However, our company has appointed me to this position and to carry out my responsibilities, I'll require the same co-operation you gave Bill in the past.'*

The next step is critical as well. Look at each person you're addressing and ask, *'Mary, can I count on you to give me the same co-operation?'* Watch Mary's body language to determine whether you can expect trouble in the future. If she shrugs her shoulders, smiles and says, *'Sure,'* you're not likely to have problems with her in the future. Ask every employee the same question and observe the responses. Their body language (be it their body position, facial expressions or tone of voice) will tell you whether you can expect trouble.

The supervisor would explain, *'Although I have worked with all of you, I don't really know the full function of your positions. Therefore, I will be having a meeting with each of you in the next two weeks so I know precisely what your responsibilities are.'* At those meetings the supervisor would discuss the job description of the person and ask about their career aspirations. For staff that seemed to still be upset about not getting the promotion, s/he would say, *'Is there anything I can do to make this transition easier for you?'* Then could add: *'I will do everything I can to prepare you for the next promotional opportunity.'*

If the employee still balks and tries to make life miserable for you, start the disciplinary procedure to ensure that their productivity and behaviour improves. Otherwise their negative behaviour may contaminate the rest of your staff.

The Human Resources person will then make sure that the new supervisor has access to her new subordinate's personnel files. S/he will also ensure that the new supervisor knows how the disciplinary procedure works in the company and offer any help the supervisor needs to fulfil this part of his/her job. Next s/he will help the new supervisor understand that things have changed now that s/he has been promoted.

The Human Resources person would then ask: *'Should you be socialising with your new staff?'*

Many will say, *'Yes.'* And you can, except you must impose a rule - no discussing business while socialising. However, if you socialise with only one of your staff - what are the rest of them thinking? They might be assuming that the employee you see socially will receive favouritism from you. You must weigh the pros and cons of continuing this kind of friendship. It's also important for you to realise that you now have a new peer group and that peer group is other supervisors.

The best solution is to gradually wean yourself away from your former peer group. You're now in the position where you must discipline your former peers the same as you would any staff you supervise. Be ready psychologically to do so by placing some distance between you and your new staff.

Sometimes supervisors pick a 'pet' employee who seems to 'get away with murder' while another (that they can't get along with) gets blamed for trivial and unimportant things. You must always be seen as unbiased by every employee you supervise. Unless all the staff members are treated equally, they may think the new supervisor is treating a staff member with favouritism or is biased against them. So think carefully about this.

Differences between counselling and disciplinary interviews:

A dual approach to discipline is recommended; that of counselling and disciplinary interviews. Normally a counselling interview is sufficient, providing it's done soon enough and the problem hasn't escalated beyond repair. This leaves pure disciplinary interviews (much harder interviews) for chronic, repeat or serious offences.

Interview Objectives:

See which step you forget during counselling or disciplinary interviews:

1. Clarify the problem. *'Joe, you've been late for work three times in the past two weeks - on May 4th, the 8th and the 13th.'*
2. Make sure there's agreement as to what the actual problem is. *'Do you agree that you were late those three dates?'* (In this case you should have time cards or facts to prove they were late, in case they deny this fact.)
3. Gain the employee's participation and commitment to solving the problem. *'What do you think you can do to be on time in the future? Can I count on you to do this?'* Notice that you're concentrating on starting good behaviour (positive) rather than on stopping bad behaviour (negative).
4. Consequences if the behaviour continues. *'I'll have to place a written warning on your file if you don't correct this problem immediately.'*

Interview pointers:

At any type of interview where you have to discuss behaviour or need to criticise others:

1. Focus on the problem; not the employee.
2. Don't try to get the employee to admit that s/he's wrong.
3. Listen to the employee.
4. Stress that you need the employee's help

5. Don't push for an immediate solution if it's not possible.
6. Consider only those ideas suggested by the employee that are usable and appropriate.

Where should interviews be held?

The issue of 'Territory' is important when you're dealing with discipline. A person has an 'edge' when they're in their own territory or on their own 'turf.' When conducting a counselling interview try to find as non-threatening an environment as possible to conduct your interviews. This would be:

First Choice: At employee's work station (providing you can have privacy) or
Second Choice: A neutral territory such as the coffee room, empty office or boardroom.
Last Choice: Your office (very threatening to the employee).

You want to have the edge at disciplinary interviews, so conduct these kinds of meetings:

- In your office.
- If person is very timid or likely to get emotional, make the environment less threatening like a neutral territory. Your second choice could be to sit on chairs facing each other or at a round table of some sort.
- If that's not available - at your desk, with them sitting at the side of the desk.
- If the situation is more serious, have him/her sit across the desk from you.
- If it's extremely serious (and you require a power base) have him/her sit in a chair lower than yours or if you're of small stature (or a woman disciplining a larger man) stand up while s/he's sitting down.

Before explaining the method I recommend, it's important for all readers to determine the way their companies handle discipline. If you work in a unionised environment, there may be different methods of how you're to conduct disciplinary interviews. This section is mainly for those who work in non-union or smaller companies where discipline may not have cut-and-dried policies and procedures set down on how to handle discipline.

148

Counselling interviews

Counselling interviews are informal interviews that deal with minor performance or behavioural problems. It's considered a verbal warning, but supervisors should document the interview in case further action is warranted. These interview notes are kept in a confidential file for the supervisor's eyes only. They do not go on the employee's personnel file because it's not a written warning. However, if the incident escalates, copies may later be attached to more formal reprimands where documentation is placed on the employee's personnel file (written warnings).

When are counselling interviews warranted?

You would use counselling interviews to deal with the following problems:

- Safety procedures aren't being followed (only if you're not sure employee knows the rules). If they know the rule is a condition of employment and break those rules, the penalty could be as severe as immediate dismissal.
- Employee shows prejudice against a peer or client;
- Production slow-down or sloppy work;
- Personality clashes;
- Abuse of work hours or coffee breaks, etc.

If done properly, counselling interviews correct minor problems. They open the door to effective communication between the employee and supervisor. It's possible that the employee didn't know their performance or behaviour was a problem or that they're breaking a company rule or regulation. A counselling interview will enlighten these employees.

Difficult counselling interviews:

Occasionally counselling interviews can be difficult ones. A supervisor notices that an employee is snarling at other employees or observes that an employee seems lethargic and his/her job performance is below normal. The supervisor calls the employee in for a counselling interview. When asked, *'What's the matter,'* the curt reply may be, *'It's none of your business!'*

What would you reply if you were his/her supervisor? You should say, *'Yes it is. Whenever your behaviour affects your* *productivity or those around you, it **is** my business.'* Then encourage the employee to discuss the problem.

If s/he still refuses add, *'You have two choices. Give me a chance to help you with your problem or get along better with your workmates and improve your job performance (or whatever was the problem). Which have you decided to do?'*

Wait for an answer. Then, let them know that you expect their behaviour to improve and give the consequences if they are not willing to change.

What do you do if the person gives you the 'silent treatment?' State your perception of the problem and allow the person to think about it. State your expectations, but keep the door open for further discussions when the employee has cooled down. This will allow the employee to settle his/her own temper and be less emotional and angry when you decide to settle the issue.

Other personal problems may surface at this kind of interview:

- family break-up
- alcoholism
- drug abuse
- illness in the home
- problems with children
- problems with spouse
- elderly parents living with them

How would you deal with these problems? Are you qualified to handle them? In most cases - no. This is why supervisors should keep abreast of where people can go to obtain counselling to solve these kinds of problems. Help them obtain this help, then back off. Make allowances on the job if necessary, but eventually stick to performance issues. Remain objective. Keep emotions in check. It's difficult to think and respond to an employee's need, if you react with emotion yourself.

Keep in mind that the problem is the other person's - don't take responsibility for it. Do however try to help him/her get through the problem. When dealing with issues of this kind, confidentiality is a must! Don't discuss these issues with others unless they're critical to solving the problem.

What do you say if an employee brings others' behaviour into the discussion?

For instance, *'Joe does that all the time - why are you picking on me?'*

Your answer should be, *'We're here to discuss your performance - not Joe's.'* You should then:

- State your perception of the problem and allow the person to think about it.
- State your expectations and keep the door open for further discussions when the employee has cooled down. This will allow the employee to settle his/her temper and be less emotional or angry when s/he decides to deal with the issue.

When you call an employee in to discuss a behaviour or production problem, keep in mind what you wish to accomplish. Let's assume that the employee requires an interview. Here's how you plan an interview (whether it is a counselling or disciplinary interview):

Planning a counselling interview:

1. Make Reference Notes to use during the interview and keep track of pertinent facts of the case. Feel free to refer to your notes and tell the employee that you'll be taking notes during the interview.
2. Make sure you have all the necessary information required to back up your claims.
   o To deal with excessive absenteeism, you'd need attendance records.
   o For a performance problem, you'd need examples of work done or production output.
3. Plan the sequence of the interview. Make sure you know the questions you need to ask to gain the necessary information.
4. Confirm privacy. This is of utmost importance when conducting this type of interview. Regardless of the nature of the problem, employees will feel far more comfortable and open if they can speak freely. Their comfort zone will lower drastically if they're worried about interruptions and/or other people over-hearing your conversation.

5. Use of hearsay information. Are you allowed to use second-hand information? What if another person said she saw Sally shopping the day she said she was away from work because of illness? Unless this employee was willing to sign a statement that she actually did see the person shopping, don't use this information. Instead, when you call the person in for the interview, ask, *'Why were you absent on Thursday?'*

   If she says, *'I was sick,'* look them in the eye and say, *'Are you sure you were ill that day?'* Because the employee will have the suspicion that you already know they weren't away because of illness, many will confess that it was a day they wanted off for other reasons. If they don't confess, you'll have to watch subsequent absences and if they become chronic, ask for a doctor's certificate for every illness.

   On the other hand, if it was you who saw her shopping when she was supposed to be away because of illness, feel free to use the information on the interview.

6. Allow enough time to conduct interviews properly. Unexpected issues may take more time to resolve than you anticipated.

7. Decide where to hold the interview. Choose the proper environment to suit the severity of the problem.

Note: The above steps may not be possible if you're faced with having to conduct an interview spontaneously. These situations occur when:

- asked for by the employee
- you notice the employee is visibly upset
- employee broke important company rules

Conducting a counselling interview:

Until you're very comfortable in conducting this kind of interview, it's recommended that you take a list of these steps with you to the interview. Don't be afraid to refer to them. It will help you obtain the objectives of the interview and keep you on track if the employee throws a 'curve' during the interview.

1. As you perceive it, state the performance or behaviour discrepancy or company rule being broken.

2. Ask the employee to verify that this is indeed the problem.
3. Ask the employee why the problem exists.
4. Ask the employee what affect this action will have on others in the area (if applicable). This is a powerful interviewing tool. Many don't use it because it results in a 'guilt trip' for the employee. Use it if they appear oblivious of the affect their performance or behaviour has on others in the area.
5. Ask the employee what s/he has attempted to do so far, about the problem.
6. Ask the employee what else s/he had considered doing and what the consequences would have been?
7. Ask the employee, *'How do you think you could solve this problem?'*
8. Ask the employee, *'How can I help?'* (Optional)
9. Get the employee's commitment to the agreed upon course of action.
10. Make sure that the employee is aware of the consequences if the unacceptable behaviour or performance continues.
11. Summarise the interview by stating your perception of the problem, your expectations and necessary guidelines.
12. Document the interview (hand written notes - do *not* put on personnel file).
13. Follow up

Documentation:

Interview notes are essential in case the problem escalates and it becomes necessary for you to conduct a more serious disciplinary interview. Follow the instructions given on how to document disciplinary interviews. At the moment, this documentation does not go on the person's personnel file – instead, they remain in your own confidential files.

Most supervisors have a confidential file, where they keep information handy for easy reference for when they do performance appraisals. This information would include special projects the employee completed, performance above and beyond the call-of-duty, problems with attendance, any counselling sessions they've had with them, etc.

Follow up:

The follow-up is very important. Along the way, you may follow-up informally. For instance: If an employee has been coming late to work, being at their work station and saying *'Good Morning,'* will keep tabs on the employee. At some time however, commend them on the positive change in their behaviour.

If the problem warrants a follow-up, set an appointment to discuss the matter - usually within two weeks or a month (whatever suits the situation). Or you may wish to set this up at the time of the counselling interview. Then ask yourself:

1. Did the employee do what s/he originally planned?
2. If s/he didn't - why not?
3. If employee did do what s/he originally planned, was s/he successful?
4. If solution didn't work - why not?
5. What other suggestions can you make and follow through?

Questioning employees:

Your role in supervisory counselling consists of these three steps:

1. Helping the individual recognise the realities s/he must deal with.
2. Assisting in identifying problem areas.
3. Demonstrating your support and assistance in helping them change.

Supportive Questions:

To perform this role effectively (especially steps 2 and 3) requires frequent use of supportive questioning. These comments show acceptance and understanding of the feelings of the person we're talking to (empathy). They show your willingness to be of aid in his/her efforts to grow and change.

Examples:

1. *'You feel that you're not getting co-operation from ...'*
2. *'How can I help you get this roadblock removed?'*
3. *'You seem to be saying that you feel you're capable in this area.'*

Exploratory Questions:

These responses are made to encourage further examination of an area even though the facts may be unpleasant. The intent of these questions is to encourage mutual problem-solving.

Examples:

1. *'Tell me more about that.'*
2. *'What seems to be the difficulty here?'*
3. *'When did this first start?'*
4. *'How does this relate to your performance?'*

Judgmental Questions:

These are responses of an evaluative type where we pass judgement upon what we've been listening to.

Examples:

1. *'You should have done ...'*
2. *'Have that finished by 3 o'clock.'*
3. *'That's a good idea.'*
4. *'That doesn't seem like much of a problem.'*

The judgemental response is the type most frequently used by supervisors (and usually appropriately so) when working with employees. In counselling situations, judgmental listening is not very desirable because too often it hampers open communication.

Maintaining improved performance:

If you want your employees to keep up their changed behaviour or performance, you would have a meeting and:

1. Describe the improved performance.
2. Explain the importance of this improvement to you and the employee's work group.
3. Listen empathetically to the employee's comments.
4. Ask the employee if there's anything you can do to make it easier for him/her to do the job.
5. If appropriate, tell employee how you're going to help him/her.
6. Thank the employee for the improved performance.

When no improvement is clear:

1. Describe the situation and review the previous discussions.
2. Ask for reasons for the situation.
3. Listen and respond with empathy.
4. Identify what action you must take (written warning, suspension, termination) and why.

5. Agree on specific action and follow up date.
6. Show your confidence in the employee.

Under no circumstances use a 'wait and see' attitude, because you're the ultimate one who will look bad if you don't act now.

CHAPTER EIGHT

DISCIPLINE PROBLEMS

Here are some of the more common reasons why supervisors must conduct counselling and disciplinary interviews:

Absenteeism:

Many employees will go to work even with a runny nose and a fever. They refuse to take advantage of their company's sick pay policy and don't wish to take sick leave for minor ailments. They feel they may need this leave when they're really sick. Others feel that no one else can handle their job as well as they can and feel responsible for their performance. To them, it's part of the ethic of being a good worker. The supervisor should recognise the sacrifices made by this kind of worker. When that type of employee is away because of illness, s/he's usually too sick to perform any kind of work at all.

Other employees will be out for any and every minor ailment. They view sick leave as their right and want to take full advantage of the accrued leave. They demonstrate little responsibility for any required productivity. The fact that other workers may have to carry a larger workload or that their company will suffer economically is of little concern to them.

A large contributor to the breakdown of employee morale, is the fact that some employees get away with calling in sick, get paid for the day and weren't the least bit ill. While it's difficult to determine completely who's truly ill and who isn't, steps can be taken that will tend to ensure that the privilege of sick leave with pay is not completely abused.

Employee absenteeism disrupts the flow of work, causes delays and production problems. The quality of work suffers because tired employees are forced to work overtime to take up the slack or the absent employee is replaced by others not as well trained.

On any normal working day, 4 to 6 per cent of all employees are usually absent from work! Does this surprise you? Because of this, supervisors must:

157

a. Enforce company rules, otherwise employee will continue abusing them and encourages others to do so as well.

b. Determine if there are absenteeism patterns.

c. Make sure employees know that being paid while they're away sick is a privilege, not a right they have as an employee and that this privilege can be removed at any time if it's being abused.

There are five major absentee reasons. Some solutions given may not agree with your company's union agreements. Check before acting to make sure you're aware of these:

1. Chronic Absentee

The person over-slept or could be a negative thinker. Everyday frustrations and pressures easily overwhelm this type of person. S/he consistently has unwarranted absences which usually follow a pattern.

How many times a year do employees pull that line before you consider them chronic absentees? One company identifies problem employees if they have eight or more absences or one or more days each month in a year.

This type of employee calls and says, *'Sorry boss, but I can't make it in today.'* You may reply, *'I'm sorry you're sick - stay away until you're feeling better.'* However, don't say that. Don't worry - the chronic absentee will stay out until they feel a lot better. Why should they have to knock themselves out? They view their sick leave as their right.

For those suspected of abusing this benefit, the supervisor should call the employee at the end of each workday. Say, *'Orson, how're you coming along? I'm calling to see if you expect to be back to work tomorrow.'*

Using this tactic allows two beautiful spin-off benefits to happen. First, you've determined that the absent employee is really at home. Of course s/he could have been at the doctor's, but every time you called him/her? Second, you'll discourage the employee from taking sick leave for minor ailments or to accomplish personal chores.

When this type of employee returns to work, the supervisor should:

a) State, *'Sure missed you yesterday. We really need and depend on you.'*
b) Describe the problems his/her absence caused the department.
c) Encourage employee to be in more often.
Explain the consequences should his/her behaviour continue.

Where the company is faced with the problem of employees who've been absent from work for excessive periods of time (i.e. chronic absenteeism) they may be discharged if they're unable to demonstrate that it's unreasonable for the employment relationship to continue. In such cases:

a) The employer must be able to document the employee's absences. These absences must be well beyond what any reasonable person would consider acceptable (keep accurate records for comparisons). The employee must have deviated substantially and unduly from the average level of attendance of other employees.
b) The employer must be able to demonstrate that the excessive absenteeism problem has been persistent. It must have continued despite documented attempts by the employer to have it corrected. The supervisor must document his/her efforts to counsel the employee and determine underlying reasons for absences. They must be able to show that s/he has shown compassion and has taken into account extenuating circumstances.
c) The employer must be able to present convincing reasons explaining why s/he feels there's little or no likelihood of improvement. The employer provides medical evidence to support this conclusion.

2. Goof-off Absentee

These people go golfing instead of doing what they consider dull, repetitious work that they feel wastes their talents and abilities. They have the need to escape the hum drum environment of work, so escape to the golf course or shopping. This can be a vicious circle. They're seldom considered for the promotion they think they need and deserve because of their excessive absenteeism. To help them lose this need to escape, the supervisor should:

a) Confront them with their absenteeism record.
b) Ask why it's happening?
c) Encourage employee to use absences properly. Explain that sick leave is a privilege, not a right and used only for their own authentic illnesses. Employers have no obligation to provide this benefit (unless stipulated clearly in union agreements or employee handbooks). Sick leave is not to be used for their children's or spouses illnesses or for personal reasons unless this coverage is included in sick leave *policies and procedures.*
d) Make sure employees are made aware that their absenteeism record is the major factor that's keeping them from being considered for a promotion.
e) Supervisor should show rewards (a promotion) that they may obtain with good attendance. This is far better than using punishment (written warning on file) to bring about positive changes in behaviour.

3. Naive Absentee

Many employees believe that management expects and condones phoney absences. These employees also believe that if they have sick leave coming, they have the right to take it whenever they please. While it's difficult to determine completely who is truly ill and who isn't, supervisors should make sure that sick leave isn't abused. To deal with this type of absentee employee, supervisors should:

a) Confront employees regarding their absenteeism record.
b) Explain what sick leave is all about (privilege not a right).
c) Tell them they're doing important work and the company suffers when they're away.
d) Encourage employees to use absences properly; for legitimate illnesses.
e) Ask employees what affect their absence could have or has had on other employees.

4. Abusive Absentee

Some employees will be out for any and every minor ailment. They demonstrate little responsibility for any required productivity. That other workers have to carry a larger workload or that their company will suffer economically is of little concern to them. This person is usually unhappy, feels victimised and believe that others receive favouritism. They break company rules and have many conflicts with their supervisors. They pick fights and believe they're always right (others are always wrong). If you have to deal with this kind of employee:

a) Threaten them with the comment, *'Your job's on the line unless you conform to the rules of this company.'*
b) Compliment them on the work they *do* when they *are* conforming to the rules.
c) Tell them they must produce doctor's reports for their absenteeism and you'll have to replace them if their record doesn't improve. Be firm and clear, sticking to the facts and the consequences if their negative behaviour continues.

5. Legitimate Absentee

These are for authentic illnesses, dentist and doctor's appointments. These employees are rarely away. Employers are willing to pay sick leave for legitimate illnesses, but should not pay for absences because of family illnesses. This should be time off without pay unless company policy states otherwise.

What would you do if a female employee explained her absences are because *of 'Female problems?'* Or, *'I have pre-menstrual tension, so need that time off every month.'* Would you know what to reply?

Reply the same way you would with any chronic illness - ask her if she's seen a doctor about her problems and that you expect her to find some solutions to the problems. In this age of enlightened medicine, it's seldom required that women use this as an authentic excuse.

Absenteeism policies:

Innocent absenteeism, even if it's excessive, doesn't warrant disciplinary action. On the other hand, an employee's inability to report regularly for work, for whatever reasons, provides grounds for termination of employment.

In industries where there's a heavier reliance on individual performance and any absence is a disruption in the flow of service to customers, management has to rely a little more on stiffer illness verification procedures including the following:

1. Requiring a doctor's certificate for three or more consecutive sick days.
2. Asking for a doctor's certificate for any absence due to illness before or after a holiday weekend.
3. Employee must complete physical examination by the company doctor if they're out more than ten days in any one year.

Falsifying a doctor's certificate should result in the employee receiving a written warning on their file and in some cases termination. The degree of discipline depends on the circumstances of each case.

Overlong lunch hour:

Abuses such as washing up and preparing for the break and getting organised after the actual break, add up to a lot of extra time lost from production. In addition, the actual time off the premises or at the cafeteria seems to grow when no effort is made to monitor this abuse.

While a supervisor may close his/her eyes to the lost time as being of small consequence, the few employees who get away with the extended lunches will cause adverse effects on employee morale. It's always better not to hedge. Get to the issue - no game-playing. The supervisor should confront them openly and tell them/they're abusing their lunch hour.

After lunch, the supervisor should be available to assess late employees. Several discipline possibilities exist, including docking for lateness, minimising overtime and changing the hour for lunch for some of the employees who are presenting a problem.

'Marty, I see you're still having difficulty getting back on the job at one o'clock. Starting tomorrow, let's try having your lunch hour start at twelve thirty and see if that's better.'

How can one expect other employees to be attentive to the lunch-hour time requirements when some of the employees get away with extended lunch hours?

Coffee break abuses:

Most companies allow fifteen minutes in the morning and afternoon for allotted coffee breaks. Studies indicate that some sort of break in the work schedule increases production. Some firms permit their employees to have their coffee and snacks at their work stations or desks. No particular time is set for the break and it tends to fit into the normal flow of work. Any congregating is discouraged. Many employees don't want to interrupt their flow of work, either because they use the more slack moments for the snack or because they may not care to have something to eat.

The second type is a work stopping time where everyone congregates in one area, such as a lunchroom or cafeteria. Supervisors must discourage employees from slowing down in anticipation of the coffee break. At the conclusion of the break, the resumption of work must be commenced otherwise the fifteen minute coffee break can extend by five minutes beforehand and then five minutes afterward (bathroom break). The management personnel could be visible immediately before and after the coffee break. They can make direct observation of abuses and encourage more productive use of time. Handing out assignments, checking on progress and other supervisory functions can be accomplished prior to and right after the break.

Despite efforts, some employees will look upon the coffee break as an opportunity to socialise and waste time. Only the conscientious effort on the part of the management personnel to observe abuses and restrict excessive break activity will cause the segregation of those who occasionally abuse, from those who will consistently abuse the time allotted.

Smoke Break Abuses:

The length of smoke breaks must comply with the company's allotted coffee and lunch break times. Most companies now have implemented 'no smoking' laws on their premises and many buildings do not allow smoking near the premises. Therefore smokers are forced to smoke outside the buildings where they work. In some cases that too is illegal so smokers sometimes have to go great distances to be able to smoke.

However, they must abide by their company's rules regarding coffee and work breaks and can be penalised for smoking on the premises or if they take longer than the allotted break times.

Personality conflicts:

If two employees don't get along, the one who usually suffers the most is their supervisor. Bob and George may be great workers, however they may be harassing each other or failing to co-operate. If the conflict is the result of a work-related cause, the supervisor will have to put his/her foot down and help the employees resolve their disagreement.

But frequently, the root cause is something related to the basic nature of the two personalities involved. That makes it a more difficult problem for the supervisor. No matter how clever the supervisor may be, s/he can't change anyone's personality. The most that s/he can hope is to get the two employees to function together in the work environment despite their admitted personality differences.

One typical method is to call both parties into a private office, let each of them state what they think the problems are (blow off a little steam) and then act as an impartial mediator whose only interest is to keep up production. The employees must know that you will not tolerate the situation remaining as it is.

Employees should be encouraged to discuss ways of resolving the problem and agree on a course of corrective action. The supervisor keeps a close watch on the situation and initiates further interviews if warranted.

Buck passing employees:

It's hard to imagine many people taking the full blame for their own errors. However, in our more complex environment, it's becoming increasingly important to avoid even minor errors.

Buck passing is often caused by a supervisor's failure to properly delegate responsibility. Procedures and policies defining responsibility were not set down in writing and/or there's a lack of an up-to-date job description. If not handled correctly, buck passing can lead to lying, cheating and burying of mistakes so that no one will find them.

The concealment of operating mistakes causes irreparable harm to the company. Service failures can be costly in the short-term and long-term dollars. Firstly, there's the cost of the immediate replacement of the service. Secondly, the quality image of the company is impaired so the ultimate sales or services are reduced. The responsibility definition for each employee is not limited to job training

'Walter, you're responsible for correctly matching the freight bills to the duplicate of the receiving report.'

'What if there are differences?'

'It's part of your duty to note the differences on the voucher to Accounts Payable. Any mistakes in matching will be your fault. Any questions?'

Even if Walter is very suited to the job, he'll still make occasional mistakes. However, he will make fewer and fewer mistakes and won't attempt to pass the buck on occasion, if he's reminded of his responsibility and if he is not over-disciplined for errors that do occur. Over-disciplining may result in excuses such as:

'The dispatcher said it's okay to approve trucking bills, so I thought this was okay too.'

'Don't blame me for that one! John said that it was okay to approve it.'

Setting an example is important. Supervisory personnel can discourage buck passing by employees if, from time to time (in the presence of their subordinates) they admit to making mistakes themselves. Certainly not every mistake needs to be admitted in front of subordinates - however, the admission of an occasional goof on the part of the supervisor demonstrates to others that passing the buck is not desirable.

Bottleneck employees:

'The work isn't getting out because George isn't doing his part!'

Bottlenecks are a frequent management complaint. But the causes are attributable to either the management's design of the workflow or to the employee's habits. Management's poor design of the workflow can be detected by a simple test. Have another employee assume the duties of the employee in the problem area.

If there is still a bottleneck (after the training period) then changes may have to be made in the workflow arrangement.

Here are the typical characteristics of a bottleneck employee:

1. Poor time management;
2. They're perfectionists;
3. Too many items held up because of relatively minor problems;
4. Not enough training;
5. Low decision-making capability;
6. Unaware of supervisor's expectations;
7. Square peg in round hole; lack of teamwork skills;
8. Job insecurity;
9. Unusual fear of making mistakes;
10. Personality clashes - lack of co-operation.

Where there's no indication that the employee is being a deliberate bottleneck, some additional on-the-job training may be in order. During this re-training, the supervisor can see if the employee understands his/her job responsibilities. S/he can demonstrate to the employee how to perform the various tasks and then guide him/her under direct observation. Little techniques that speed the job along should be emphasised.

The employee should learn how his/her job fits into the total picture and what contribution s/he's expected to make. If employees are more aware of what functions are performed before or after theirs, they can use their judgement and understand the consequences of their own performance.

Most 'sticks-in-the-mud' don't really want to be 'sticks-in-the-mud.' Nearly everyone wants to feel that s/he is co-operating in achieving common goals. The ploy is to make everyone in the work force have a common goal.

Other employees can be encouraged to assist:

'Say Tom, can you show Dick how he can move that project faster?'

'Dick, let Tom show you a couple of techniques for pushing the stuff through that we need now.'

Encourage the problem employee to want to put the work out faster. The paying of a few compliments here and there improves confidence among slower employees. It permits them to have a greater feeling of job security and certainly reduces tensions. The bottleneck employee can become less fearful of incidental mistakes, thus reducing his/her own built-in need for more control on his/her work.

Aggressive attitude:

The experienced supervisor knows which employees have feelings of aggression toward their work situation. The feelings which cause the aggressive attitude are deep-rooted and the supervisor has the problem of either changing them (which admittedly is difficult) or re-directing them to the advantage, not only for the company, but for the employee as well. Some job related causes of aggressive behaviour on the part of employees could include:

1. Insecurity on the job.
2. Employee's lack of qualifications or credentials.
3. Little recognition of employee's achievements.
4. Under-utilisation of their abilities.
5. Lack of acceptance with work groups (including racial and cultural differences).
6. Failure to feel settled into their occupation.

Those who don't believe they fit into their positions are likely to act aggressively towards supervisors, the company, top management, the job, fellow workers and their immediate boss. Some effort can be made to direct their negative attitudes of aggression toward a work related goal even if their attitude can't be changed. Techniques used by a supervisor may be to:

1. Show employees how their efforts affect their fellow workers. Explain how their jobs are important to their company.
2. Make problem employee feel secure in their job.
3. Indicate that with their training and other qualifications, they have the capability to do more than a satisfactory job.
4. Give recognition more frequently to aggressive-tendency employees.

5. Bring them into group conversations: ask for their advice.
6. Identify their responsibilities and set performance standards.

If the supervisor's attitude indicates that s/he feels the problem employee has much to contribute to the entire group's productivity, the employee is likely to assume such a role. Most aggressive employees are very success-oriented. Their drive for recognition could cause the employee to set high goals for him/herself in order to achieve further recognition.

Channelling this energy in the right direction can be a major step in the right direction for this type of employee.

Ethnic problems:

Most work forces, if they're in compliance with the law, are a mixture of individuals of different ethnic backgrounds. Turning the other cheek or tolerating an ethnic slur, whether against an employee, a supervisor, a customer or someone in the general public, shows poor management. An ethnic slur is destructive of the public good portion of the company image and can undo the efforts put into the human relations among employees.

Jokes at the expense of someone else are not jokes at all!

Sometimes the 'joke' telling gets out of hand and someone's feelings are hurt. Comments or 'jokes' should be discouraged as soon as someone starts, *'Did you hear the one about the ...?'*

Supervisors should never knowingly joke about someone's background or personal appearance, nor should they condone such behaviour on the part of their employees. One can't judge on the surface how a joke in poor taste might affect an individual. Ethnic comments stem from prejudice and not from facts. Prejudice presumes that there is a stereotype of an ethnic group and disregards its members as individuals with different characteristics. Use such reminders as:

'I didn't think that was funny, Paul.'

This shows your disapproval and makes the employees more aware that you're monitoring such kinds of jokes. A supervisor's put down of a slurring joke should be indicative of top management's attitude towards any kind of prejudice.

Sometimes a private session with the offender is necessary. The supervisor should deal with these 'harmless' remarks immediately.

'Charlie, these remarks might appear to be harmless to you, but they may not appear that way to the receiver of your comments. Keep those kinds of comments to yourself.'

If the problem continues - the supervisor should say: *'Charlie, a note is made on each performance appraisal on how you get along with the other employees (or customers, etc.). I wouldn't like to place a comment on your personnel record that you don't get along - but that's what I'll have to do if you keep making those remarks that I warned you about - do you understand?'* Or, conduct a formal disciplinary interview explaining the consequences to Charlie if he continues to act as he has in the past.

Personal telephone calls

Nothing is as annoying to a supervisor as watching a particular employee receiving an excessive number of personal telephone calls. It's not just that the lines are being tied up, but the employee's flow of work is also interrupted. An employee's personal calls should be held to a minimum. After all, s/he is at a place of business - his/her personal requirements should be able to wait until coffee or lunch break or after work.

One thing you could tell the employee is:

'Sally, when you use company time to conduct personal business - whether it is a telephone call, gossiping or just discussing what you did on the weekend - you're using part of my department's budget without anything productive coming in. Can you see that if you continue doing this, I'll be forced to overlook you for a promotion? I can't afford the time and production wastage. If I promoted you and paid you more money, I certainly wouldn't be able to afford that wastage.'

Or, your company could:

1. Consider installing Voice Mail:
2. Ask them to advise their friends and relatives about the company policy. Reserving the phones for important or

emergency calls may not eliminate the frivolous calls entirely, but it will make fair minded employees follow the rules. If your company does not have voice mail, you might also:

3. Require the receptionist to ask an incoming caller for his/her name and say, *'What company do you represent?'* Nothing further needs to be ventured by the receptionist. The question may be enough to embarrass the caller without being too nosy. Such a question tends to reduce the calls and their duration. Or the receptionist might keep track of such calls for one or two days and submit the report to the supervisor of each section. Follow-up by having interviews with employees who are still abusing the telephone.

Mistake-ridden employees:

Just as auto insurance companies recognise that some drivers are more prone to having accidents than the general population of drivers, some recognition must be given to the fact that some employees are more likely to make mistakes than others. Of course, deliberate mistakes are a cause for the use of disciplinary measures, up to and including firing the errant employee. However, most mistakes are not intentional. They're caused by a variety of reasons, including errors in judgement on the part of management.

There are two basic kinds of mistakes; system mistakes and human mistakes. The first results from the design of a system. Constant improvement of the system will reduce the error rate.

No matter how well the system is designed, there is a certain amount of reliance on the human factor. That factor is the one to which line management personnel have to apply a great deal of attention. The system's designer may also be at fault for the 'human' mistakes to occur. Some of the following conditions may also exist:

1. Inadequate job training.
2. Limited written instructions.
3. Large number of subordinates reporting to one supervisor (12 should be maximum).
4. Too few intermediate levels of management.
5. Dull work environment.
6. Job boredom.

7. Poor analysis of error cause.
8. High employee turnover.

Most employees like to feel that they're earning their pay. Part of that feeling of pride stems from their opinion that their work has few, if any, errors. Therefore, they appreciate help, when offered gracefully, in improving their own image of pride in their work. One method is to provide an employee/coach for the error prone employee.

A senior employee who's proficient in his/her job, will be able to isolate the causes of the problem employee's errors and provide instruction in special techniques to either avoid such errors or catch the mistakes and take corrective action. To minimise carelessness, the problem employee has to be shown at which points in the process, some additional attention should be applied:

'Arnold, could you spend a little more time rechecking your work?'
'Donna, can you pay a little more attention to these types of items?'

To summarise:
1. Determine the nature of errors.
2. Revise your system to improve error detection.
3. Use a senior employee as a coach to an error prone employee.
4. Consider employee's pride of workmanship.
5. Have a chat with an error prone employee to review causes of mistakes.

When to interfere in personal employee problems:

Personal problems of various kinds interfere in many ways with an employee's performance at work, including:

1. High absentee record.
2. Requests to leave work early.
3. Lateness at the start of work and around coffee and lunch breaks.
4. High number of personal telephone calls.
5. High error rate and breaking of company or safety rules.
6. Little response to group effort.

7. Reduced production.
8. Increased fatigue.
9. Reduced availability for overtime.
10. High 'Sickness' days out.
11. Loss of initiative.
12. Expressions of irritability to co-workers.
13. Requests for irregular vacation time.
14. Antagonism toward supervisor.
15. Lower training capability.
16. Low company loyalty.
17. High grievance rate.

Confidentiality is important. The employee should be advised that the matter will go no further than the supervisor. The supervisor can point out the extent to which the employee's performance is below average. Comparisons to previous records can be made. The supervisor can offer assistance in solving the personal problem, but s/he must stress that suitable performance from the employee must be the end result.

For instance:
'I know you're having a bad time right now Sandra, but I still need to keep up our production quotas. Can I count on you doing your share?'
'Sandra, I know that you're capable of better work. Is there some way I can help you to get back on the right track?'
'I don't know.'
'Well, Sandra, maybe I can suggest a solution. At least I'll understand what's happening, even if I can't be of any help.'

Upon becoming aware that the supervisor has noticed a change in attitude or lower performance, the employee may push to solve his/her own problem - or at least learn to live with it so that it doesn't affect his/her work.

The supervisor's duty is to assist a subordinate who has a personal problem - if such assistance is wanted and is possible. Second, there's the obligation to the company, which requires the best performance possible from each employee. The time to interfere is when the supervisor decides that s/he can accomplish both these objectives - render some assistance and maintain production. A little caution is advisable; the supervisor should not become directly involved other than as a possible source of advice.

Employee daydreaming:

We all daydream, but some people do it to excess; to a point where it interferes with work or productivity. Some jobs lend themselves more to employee daydreaming than others and have to be monitored more carefully.

It's not always fair to pin the blame for daydreaming on the employees. Their jobs may be so boring that they can't keep their minds on them. Machine-like functions tend to create opportunities for daydreaming. Where greater worker attention is required, daydreaming can result in loss of productivity, errors and even accidents. The problem may be that the job was not designed to hold the employee's attention.

The design of the work area can reduce the tendency to daydream. Operations that must be performed while standing tend to discourage daydreaming. The work area decor is of some importance. Desks or work areas need not be all the same colour. Attempts should be made to eliminate monotony in the work environment. This is why job rotation is so popular. The spin-off benefit is that more people are trained to do more jobs. Should an employee be away because of illness, there's someone already trained to take over his or her position.

Those work situations that require a higher degree of creativity on the part of the employee should have an environment that's conducive to creativity.

If there's any flexibility in the method of performing the job, add that flexibility into the operation description. This will allow the employees to decide how to handle particular steps by using their initiative in selecting their production process. Such flexibility permits employees to think about how they want to handle particular jobs and therefore increases their alertness and reduces monotony.

No matter what efforts are made in dispelling daydreaming potential, some employees seem to be lost in the clouds. Only constant management attention can dispel the problem and keep employees on their toes. Sometimes, a discussion between the supervisor and the employee is in order.

Disorganised or messy work area:

Many think that good housekeeping is not an indication of an efficient operation. They consider it window dressing, for they believe that an operation can be just as productive no matter what the housekeeping conditions are. However, some of the characteristics that do affect efficiency and are evidence of poor housekeeping include:

1. Missing records or files;
2. Lost or misplaced tools or equipment;
3. High supply costs;
4. Improper mix of parts and inventory;
5. High contamination of product;
6. High scrap and rework costs;
7. Poor balance of finished products inventory;
8. High machine down time;
9. Poor safety record;
10. Low employee morale - disinterest in working overtime;
11. Discipline problems and labour turnover.

One way of motivating employees to maintain a tidy work area is to set a good example. If the supervisor's office is neat and clean, then good housekeeping habits are more easily encouraged among the rank and file. Encourage daily clean-up at the end of the day. If the supervisor spots employees heading for the door, leaving messy work stations, s/he should stop employees and ask them to organise their work station before leaving. For more difficult problems, a written checklist of housekeeping activities is advisable.

Supply theft:

There was a time when thefts from inventory only affected industries that had 'attractive' types of inventory. Increasingly, all types of inventory are becoming subject to theft - not only completed assemblies, but parts and even raw materials are also being stolen.

Employees who take home a few coloured pencils so that their children can complete a colouring book, are setting a bad example in attitude. Some employees go far beyond a few pencils. It's not that they're kleptomaniacs, but rather, it's to get back at management. Some of these people will steal quantities far in excess of what they can ever use. To some extent, it's their way of getting around the rules and back at authority.

Usually, employees who constantly steal are poor employees, not only because of their thieving, but for other reasons as well. It's not just that they have low regard for company property, but frequently they also think little of the company for which they work.

It's not economically justifiable to lock everything up, nor is it possible to catch all the culprits, but if management removes some of the temptations, they'll have fewer losses. Having only one or more people in charge of the company office supplies etc., will cut down on pilfering. Having employees sign for stationery and equipment is another.

Alcoholic employee:

Employees who are found at work in an intoxicated state should not be allowed to drive home. Most laws insist that the company send the employee home by some other means, either with a workmate or in a taxi.

When an employee's problem of excessive absenteeism is due to a drinking problem, the employer may discharge the employee. The supervisor must be able to demonstrate that the employment relationship cannot continue. The company must be able to defend their decision and show that they have recognised the alcoholic problem as an illness. They must prove they've made an honest effort to assist employees to deal with their illness.

Experienced supervisors will advise that any promise by employees that they can control their alcoholic habit must be viewed with suspicion. Many won't admit to themselves (much less to the boss) that they have a drinking problem. This makes for a strong distinction between the alcoholic and the other types of problem employees who frequently admit to their shortcomings.

Most people drink and even though some may be considered heavy drinkers - not all become alcoholics. The few that do can be helped more successfully, if help is offered in the early stages.

Generally, the drinker who has become an alcoholic will begin to incur a high absentee record; not necessarily typified by the Monday and Friday syndrome. (Frequently they've dried out by Monday and if Friday is payday they need the cash). Partial attendance can be expected. Often related illness forces them to be late or they leave after lunch break. Sometimes food makes employees ill or they may wish to indulge their weakness.

When questioned about the absences or the partial absences, the alcoholic can't be expected to admit to the real cause, but will offer any excuse. Supervisors must realise that this kind of problem is beyond his/her realm of responsibility. Employees with this problem must be encouraged to obtain help from their family doctor, Alcohol Anonymous or any other source available to him/her. The supervisor must, however, be very firm in stating to the employee that failures in performance must be corrected and it is up to the employee to find the way to accomplish this.

A frequent attribute of the problem of the alcoholic employee is that many workmates and supervisors wish to conceal the problem. They have a desire to 'help' the employee by not permitting the higher levels of management to be aware that one of their employees is an alcoholic. For some reason, this type of cover-up is not tried with other types of problems. This is genuinely peculiar to employee alcoholism.

Some of the reasons used for covering up for the alcoholic include:

1. Charlie is a good worker;
2. He needs the job and getting caught would finish him and his family;
3. He has a lot of problems at home;
4. He would help anybody he could;
5. It's an illness that can't be cured by letting management know;
6. It will only take a short while to sober him up;
7. The job caused him to drink.

In circumstances such as these, employees may run circles around their supervisors and co-workers who mistakenly believe they can help employees by covering up their actions.

One way of overcoming the willingness to conceal the alcoholic employee is to set the record straight with regard to all alcoholics:

1. If the alcoholic employee drives to and from work or uses a company vehicle, s/he may be a deadly menace to him/herself as well as to others on the road.
2. The alcoholic is a threat to his/her own safety and that of others while on the job. If an alcoholic injures him/herself at work while intoxicated, s/he generally cannot obtain worker compensation for any job-related injury. Also: Other injured employees may not recover worker's compensation and may have to lodge a personal law suit against the alcoholic to pay for any time off because of an injury.
3. An alcoholic doesn't get cured by someone covering up for him/her. S/he continues to be a problem both at work and at home.
4. The company's community relations suffer if other organised groups in the community see a tolerance for alcoholism in the company image.
5. If an employee has customer contact while intoxicated, s/he will cause a loss of sales for the company.
6. Many employees, as well as the parents of some of the younger employees, are offended by the presence of an alcoholic employee on the premises.
7. An alcoholic can only be cured with the assistance of experienced counsellors who are skilled in such matters.
8. An alcoholic employee, besides problems with tardiness and absenteeism, may:
   a) Disregard safety rules;
   b) Be indifferent to productivity requirements;
   c) Have a higher error rate;
   d) Drink on the premises;
   e) Steal company and/or other employee's property;
   f) Encourage others to violate company rules.

Supervisors and other personnel should advise alcoholic employees that drinking is a problem that they haven't been able to handle on their own. They should explain they understand that they have a problem and will do what they can to help. While only the individual can stop the drinking, the associates should applaud the alcoholic's effort in overcoming his/her problem.

Supervisors and other management personnel should be made aware that cover-up of the existence of alcoholic employees will not be tolerated and that the company has rules with regard to the handling of employees who drink on the job. If an employee is interested in helping the alcoholic, there are ways - not by trying to cover-up for him/her, but by encouraging him/her to seek assistance.

Sexual harassment

Anyone (male or female) can experience sexual harassment, but the vast majority of these are women. It's been established that most sexual discrimination is against women. Research indicates that seventy to eighty percent of women have experienced one or more forms of sexual harassment while working. What is criminal is that fifty-two percent of these have left a job because of it!

This is one work problem that's bothered women in the workplace for centuries. However, the situation is changing slowly as laws are updated to protect women in the workplace.

Sexual harassment is unlawful, direct discrimination on the ground of sex. Harassment can produce a hostile work environment that can adversely affect the terms and conditions of employment and make it impossible for the person to continue employment.

Men sometimes discount the impact sexual harassment has on women. It could be compared in severity to a situation where a supervisor doesn't like an employee, so makes his/her job so difficult s/he is forced to leave the job. This is called workplace bullying or harassment and both men and women have suffered from it.

An employer has a legal responsibility to ensure that there are no policies or practices operating within an organisation that directly or indirectly discriminate against women. An employer can be vicariously liable for the actions of an employee even if the employer was unaware of the actual actions of the employee. All organisations have a responsibility to ensure the workplace is free from harassment of any kind

Make sure you check your local laws concerning Sexual Harassment. The Queensland, Australia Anti-discrimination Act protects everyone from unfair discrimination and sexual harassment. Both men and women are protected from unfair discrimination and sexual harassment in every aspect of their work including recruitment, hiring, job interviews, the terms and conditions on which a job is offered, employment benefits, availability of training courses, transfers, promotions and dismissal, in the lunch room, the factory or the office.

What is sexual harassment?

Sexual harassment is any form of sexual attention that is unwelcome. It may be unwelcome touching or other physical contact, remarks with sexual connotations, smutty jokes, requests for sexual favours, leering or the display of offensive material such as pictures, posters or computer graphics. Sexual harassment has nothing to do with mutual attraction. Such friendships are a private matter.

Sexual harassment can be a single incident – it depends on the circumstances. Obviously some actions or remarks are so offensive that they constitute sexual harassment in themselves, even if they're not repeated. Other single incidents such as an unwanted invitation out or compliment may not constitute harassment if they are not repeated.

There is an onus on the person being harassed to say s/he finds the conduct objectionable. Many people find it difficult to speak up. All employees are responsible for their own behaviour. If you think your behaviour may offend - then don't do it!

Sexual harassment is very serious. It is any form of unwanted, unwelcome or uninvited sexual behaviour that is or might be offensive, humiliating, intimidating or embarrassing. The law covers harassment of both men and women, whether they are employers, supervisors, co-workers or clients. It can include an unwelcome sexual advance, unwelcome request for sexual favours or other unwelcome conduct of a sexual nature. Sexual harassment has nothing to do with mutual attraction or friendship. Sexual interaction such as flirtation and attraction is not sexual harassment when it is invited, mutual, consensual or reciprocated.

Sexual harassment can take various forms and be obvious or indirect, physical or verbal. It includes behaviour that creates a sexually hostile or intimidating environment.

Specifically, examples of sexual harassment include:

- Unwelcome physical touching;
- Sexual or suggestive comments, jokes or innuendo;
- Unwelcome requests for sex;
- Intrusive questions about a person's private life;
- The display of sexually explicit material such as posters or pictures;
- Unwanted invitations;
- Staring or leering;
- Sex based insults or taunts; and
- Offensive communications, including telephone calls, letters, faxes and e-mail.

Some forms of sexual harassment, such as assault, physical molestation, stalking, sexual assault and indecent exposure, are also criminal offences and the offender may be prosecuted accordingly.

Where does sexual harassment happen?

Sexual harassment can happen anywhere - in the street, at a job interview or in the workplace. The most common places are:

- At work - by an employer, supervisor or manager, co-worker or colleague.
- In education - by a teacher, lecturer or by another student.
- In obtaining goods and services - by a shopkeeper, shop assistant, credit provider, trades person, doctor, publican, mechanic, etc.
- In accommodation and housing - by landlord or real estate agent.
- When participating in government programs - by a trainer or government worker delivering programs or services.

Who is liable for discrimination and sexual harassment?

As well as the person doing the discriminating, employers are also liable for discrimination or sexual harassment done by their employees or agents in the course of their work. Complaints can be made against either or both. No longer can others 'turn the other cheek' and walk away from acts of sexual harassment. They have an obligation to report the incident and ensure that it doesn't happen again. Employers can defend themselves against a complaint if they can show they took reasonable steps to prevent the discrimination or harassment.

Reasonable steps include the development, promotion and implementation of policies against discrimination and sexual harassment, training in these matters for staff and the establishment and promotion of grievance procedures for employees with complaints. All employers are obliged to have policies and programs in place designed to create a harassment-free workplace.

Above all, employers should take complaints seriously and deal with them promptly, sensitively and confidently. It's no defence for employers to plead ignorance of the actions of their workers or agents. Complaints can be submitted up to a year after the time of the discrimination or harassment.

How does sexual harassment affect others?

It can affect work performance and opportunities and can create a hostile or unpleasant work environment. It can make the person feel insecure and fearful about his/her housing. It can seriously affect their studies and future career or can affect access to goods and services.

Those who believe they have been sexually harassed are encouraged to lodge a complaint with the Anti-Discrimination Commission. In Australia, there are several Acts and Commissions involved. The Human Rights and Equal Opportunity Commission is a quasi-judicial tribunal which hears and determines public inquiries under the following two acts:

- Racial Discrimination Act: Makes certain acts of racial discrimination unlawful. This is a Commonwealth Act that applies throughout Australia.
- Sex Discrimination Act, 1984: Makes certain discriminatory actions on grounds of sex, marital status and pregnancy unlawful. This is a commonwealth act that applies throughout Australia.
- Anti-Discrimination Act, 1991
- Human Rights Act, 2004

I cover this topic at several of my seminars and often run into resistance from some of the male participants. Their comments are often, *'Women are coming into **our** workplace, they should have to adapt to our way of speaking and behaving - not us to theirs!'*

When asked if they'd use those kinds of comments, innuendos or sexual references in their homes, their answer is, *'Of course not, my wife would throttle me!'*

My reply to that is, *'Then why would you consider using that kind of behaviour or language in a place of business?'*

If I receive additional resistance, I ask one of the defensive participants whether they have any daughters, a girlfriend, wife or mother. Then I ask them how they would feel if their daughter, girlfriend, wife or mother was working and someone treated them in that fashion. Their response is usually, *'I'd punch his lights out!'*

They soon get the message, that the women they might be harassing probably have fathers, brothers, boyfriends or husbands who are just as offended by their behaviour towards their family members.

However, many simply did not know that such actions were against the law and therefore they must change their behaviour towards women.

Companies are encouraged to post sexual harassment policies in employee lunch or staff rooms so staff are aware that the company will not condone that kind of behaviour.

Model sexual harassment policy

(Company name) Sexual Harassment Policy

(Company name) considers sexual harassment an unacceptable form of behaviour that will not be tolerated under any circumstances. The company believes that all employees should be able to work in an environment free of intimidation and sexual harassment.

Sexual harassment may cause the loss of trained and talented employees and damage staff morale and productivity. Under the Queensland Anti-Discrimination Act and the Federal Sex Discrimination Act, sexual harassment is against the law. Supervisors and managers must ensure that all employees are treated equitably and are not subject to sexual harassment. They must also ensure that people who make complaints or are witnesses, are not victimised in any way.

Any reports of sexual harassment will be treated seriously and investigated promptly, confidentially and impartially. A written complaint is not required. Disciplinary action will be taken against anyone who sexually harasses a co-worker or client. Discipline may involve a warning, transfer, counselling, demotion or dismissal, depending on circumstances.

Workplace bullying

(See my book on this topic entitled ***Dealing with Workplace Bullying – Society's Corporate Disgrace!***)

Unfortunately, workplace Australia does not have laws in place that protect workers from workplace bullying, harassment or violence. If you do a word check on the contents of your State or Territory's Occupational Health and Safety Regulations, you will see that nowhere in the document does it discuss workplace bullying, harassment or violence. However, if the behaviour of the bully is serious enough, the victim can report the incident(s) to the police and lodge assault charges.

Many people who are guilty of workplace bullying are in positions of power and were most likely bullies at school. Workplace bullying (harassment or assault) may consist of a single traumatic incident or several incidents. It may also follow a pattern of constant fault-finding, criticising, segregating, excluding, undermining, over weeks or months.

Society makes the assumption that all bullies are male, but women can be as vicious as men. Workplace bullies often appear competent and professional at their jobs, but behind the façade, they're inadequate and inept. Some have unpredictable mood swings - they're like time bombs. They gain gratification from provoking people into emotional or irrational responses. The vulnerability of others is the primary stimulant to bullies.

Many bullies have:

- Greater-than-average aggressive behaviour patterns;
- A desire to dominate peers;
- A need to feel in control, to win;
- No sense of remorse for hurting another;
- An inability to accept responsibility for their behaviour.

Who are the targets of bullying?

Targets of bullying are assumed to be loners, but most are independent, self-reliant people who have no need for gangs or cliques, have no need to impress and are not interested in office politics. Bullies select individuals who prefer to use dialogue to resolve conflict, who have a low propensity for violence and who will go to great lengths to avoid conflict. They constantly try to use negotiation rather than resort to grievance and legal action. Targets are chosen because they're competent and popular. Bullies are jealous of the easy and stable relationships that targets have with others.

How to deal with workplace bullying

Every company should have clearly defined policies and procedures relating to workplace bullying. Review them and follow the procedures. If your company does not have one, search online or consult a lawyer, ideally one involved with labour or human rights, for information regarding the appropriate government agency to contact.

Model bullying, harassment, violence policy

(Company name) Bullying, Harassment and Violence Policy

(Company name's) policy and practice is to maintain a work environment free from unlawful discrimination and harassment. It is the right of each employee to be treated with dignity and respect and it is each employee's responsibility to treat others the same way.

(Company name) will not tolerate harassment in any form. Harassment is unlawful. It amounts to discriminatory behaviour under Federal and State anti-discrimination legislation. (Company name) will not tolerate offensive, humiliating, coercive, intimidating or harassing behaviour from anyone. This responsibility extends not only to employees, but also to all people with whom we deal in conducting our business. Any such inappropriate behaviour will be taken very seriously.

(Company name's) Objectives

(Company name) is committed to a comprehensive strategy for eliminating discrimination and harassment. We aim to:

- Create an environment where all employees and customers are treated with dignity, courtesy and respect;
- Implement training and awareness raising strategies to ensure that all employees know their rights and responsibilities;
- Provide an effective procedure for complaints based on the principles of natural justice;
- Treat all complaints in a sensitive, fair, timely and confidential manner;
- Provide protection from victimisation or reprisals;
- Encourage the reporting of behaviour which breaches this policy; and
- Promote appropriate standards of conduct at all times.

Definitions:

Harassment is a form of discrimination that occurs when a person is subjected to unwelcome, uninvited behaviour they find offensive, humiliating, embarrassing or intimidating. Harassment can take many forms and may include physical contact, verbal comments, jokes, pictures and gestures. Harassment includes many things that might not readily be perceived as harassment by everyone, but which the law says amounts to harassment. These include:

- Belittling, demeaning or patronising the victim - especially in front of others;
- Shouting at and threatening the target, often in front of others;
- Making snide comments to see if the person will fight back;

- Finding fault and criticising everything the victim says and does or twisting, distorting and misrepresenting the victim. The criticism may be of a trivial nature; but often there's a grain of truth in it that can dupe the victim into believing the criticism is valid.
- Stubbornly refuse to recognise the victim's contributions;
- Attempting to chip away at the target's status, self-confidence, worth and potential;
- Treating the victim differently - showing favouritism to others and bias toward the victim.

Application of Policy

This policy applies to all activities and all people involved in those activities (whether or not they are [Company name] employees) that take place:

- On (Company name) premises and
- Otherwise as a consequence of employment at (Company name).

CHAPTER NINE

DISCIPLINARY INTERVIEWS

Preparing yourself psychologically:

As a manager you'll face many disciplinary problems. If I anticipate an interview might be a difficult one, I rehearse the situation with a colleague of mine. The colleague plays 'Devil's Advocate' and is as difficult as he can be. In our role-playing, I'm able to try out different approaches until I find one that will work best. Then when the actual interview takes place, I'm not faced with unexpected problems.

The discipline procedure:

Here are the normal steps taken in the disciplinary procedure. Problem situations may not have all these steps. For instance: If the situation is serious enough, step 4 may be the only step taken (Always check your union agreement first before considering the following):

1. Verbal warning and counselling interview.
2. First written warning and disciplinary interview.
3. Second written warning and disciplinary interview (optional).
4. Dismissal, termination or firing (whichever term your company uses).

Disciplinary interviews:

Before conducting a disciplinary interview, be sure to prepare for it. Questions you might ask yourself are:

- When should the interview take place?
- If you have to terminate an employee, when would you choose to do so?

Most managers would agree that the discipline often has to happen when the infraction occurs. In other situations you may not have to act immediately. If that's done, choose the latter part of the day, when the employee can go home and think about the situation. If they have further work to do, it may change their concentration level or they may not produce the normal work expected of them. Termination of an employee would follow the same course. At times, the employee can be fired on the spot if the situation is serious enough (more later on this topic).

Conducting a disciplinary interview:

Take the following steps if you've preceded the disciplinary interview with a counselling interview:

1. Summarise what has taken place using any documentation that you've made before the interview.
2. Ask the employee why in his/her opinion s/he hasn't resolved the problem. Remain flexible - new information may warrant further counselling.
3. Ask the employee if there's any further information or suggestions s/he might have. Once again, this is a decision-making-point - you may decide to try the counselling approach once more in light of new information.
4. Set authoritative guidelines. For example *'Tomorrow, you must start coming in on time. We've given you every opportunity to solve your problem. If it's not solved by then, I'll have to take further action (specify).'*
5. Get the employee's agreement that s/he understands your position. Ask the employee, *'What is your understanding of the situation?'*
6. Attempt to get his/her commitment to determine a course of action which will solve the problem. Ask a question such as, *'Are you willing to try to meet my expectations?'* Be supportive, *'I know you can do it.'*
7. Be sure that the employee is aware of the consequences if the unacceptable behaviour or performance continues.
8. Document the interview.
9. Follow up within a reasonable length of time.

If this is the first disciplinary interview, leave out the steps relating to counselling interviews.

Documentation:

Disciplinary interviews are tougher to conduct than counselling interviews because written warnings have to be put on the employee's file. Take care that this documentation is accurate.

Normally, three copies are made, one for the employee, one for the supervisor, one for the employee's personnel file (and if there is a union – one for the union representative). If the employee was terminated, they might decide to start legal action and charge you and your company with wrongful dismissal. In that case, your documentation would be used in a court of law - so do it correctly!

It's important to check to see what your company normally does to document interviews. It's possible that they don't include enough information on their documentation to win a case in court.

Purpose of Documentation:

- Provides a permanent record that the interview took place.
- Provides an accurate statement in the event that it must go to a higher authority in the company or to a court of law.
- Serves as an indicator to an employee that the matter under discussion is a serious one.
- Provides an agreement for follow-up purposes at an agreed upon date.

Suggested content:

- Employee's name
- Employee's number
- Employee's position
- Supervisor's name
- Supervisor's title
- Unit or branch
- Location
- Date and time of interview
- Place of Interview
- Who at interview
- Purpose of interview
- Information given by supervisor
- Questions asked by the supervisor
- Answers and additional information given by employee
- Effect the employee's action had on others
- Course of action agreed upon
- Consequences should problem persist (discipline)

- Follow up interview date and time
- Signature of employee
- Signature of supervisor
- Signature of union representative (if required)
- Signature of any witnesses

Note: These are suggested headings - use whatever appears applicable to the situation.

Don't neglect follow-up interviews which are much more important in the case of disciplinary than counselling interviews. Set a date at the time of the initial interview.

Reasons for this are:
1. If people are doing what they're supposed to be doing, the supervisor should recognise that achievement and act accordingly.
2. If not, the supervisor must offer additional assistance or take further disciplinary action.

Who should compile this report or should it be hand written? Preferably you will prepare them on your computer and store in a confidential file. If you don't have access to a computer your Human Resources or Employee Relations department staff (who deal every day with confidential information) would be able to prepare these reports. If you hand print the information, make sure you use black pen because blue ink does not copy as well. Make sure all information stays confidential.

If the employee refuses to sign the document, insert the comments 'Employee refused to sign document.' Then give date and either initial or sign in full.

It's important to emphasise that, in documenting the interview, you record the facts of the situation not assumptions, inferences or your feelings about it! Make your notes right after the conclusion of the interview.

How long do you think written warnings should remain on an employee's personnel file? Your company probably has a set time. If it doesn't, evaluate each situation individually. If the employee has had no other problems for a year, I'd probably remove the warning from their file. Most employees feel as if a cloud is hanging over them as long as warnings are on their file. Many use tunnel-vision when performing their duties and stop taking any kind of risk. Some lower their productivity level.

On the other hand, if the employee has been in several 'scrapes' in the past year, leave warnings on his/her file. A pattern is showing up here that may lead to more serious discipline and possibly termination.

If an employee asked to see his/her personnel file, would you show it to them? By law you have to make it available to them within twenty-four hours. The employee would normally have copies of all the documentation on their file except your interview notes. This should remind you not to put anything on their personnel file that would appear as if you were discriminating against them. If viewed by the employee, they may take your interview notes describing them as biased, stereotyped or prejudiced. Clean out all employee personnel files to remove this possibility.

Types of disciplinary action:

Before deciding which kind of disciplinary action you wish to take, check to see what is the normal procedure in your company or industry. Also check union agreements and employee handbooks to see what options might be identified for infractions.

a) Written warning with consequences of further action, possibly termination
b) Suspension from work with pay
c) Suspension from work without pay
d) Demotion - be careful of this one. In many areas it's considered that if you demote an employee, you've first (unofficially) fired them and have re-hired them at a lower-level position. This would make it necessary for you to have very accurate documentation as to why you 'fired' them.
e) Transfer to another job or area
f) No promotion until behaviour warrants it
g) Termination or dismissal

Termination/dismissal/firing:

Consult with your Human-Resources Department to be sure that your reason for firing the employee is justified and within any formal company policies. If your company does not have a formal discharge policy, seek out a long-time staffer in senior management who can fill you in on common firing practices. You may also want to check with your legal department.

Make sure your reason is one that has been uniformly enforced. For example, if you object to the employee's sales performance, be sure you've enforced the same quotas for other employees. Employers have a responsibility to keep employees informed of their shortcomings before you fire them. Some companies require that another manager or a member of the Human Resources department (or union representative) be at disciplinary meetings as a witness.

Watch what you say when you speak to the employee. Don't say anything that could be interpreted as discriminatory. If you've kept the employee informed at each step - explained that their performance required improvement, given written warnings that clearly spell out what the consequences would be if their behaviour not improve - the employee can't very well blame you for terminating them. They were the ones who decided to continue with their undesirable performance or behaviour - not you.

'Dismissal for Just Cause' allows the employer to dismiss the employee summarily without providing any period of notice. This arises where the employee has repudiated an essential term of the employment contract thereby indicating that s/he no longer wishes to be bound by the contract. There are no hard and fast generalisations or rules that can be made as to what constitutes just cause.

Termination is the most drastic kind of discipline. Make sure proper documentation is completed before or immediately after termination.

Immediate dismissal:

Note: It's essential that you check your local laws, awards and agreements to make sure these apply in your area:

1. Theft of property or information - be sure you can prove this is the case!
2. Absence without leave for more than three days. It's assumed that the employee has abandoned his/her position.

3. Falsification of records or information. This could be intentional errors on time cards or lying on an employment interview or giving inaccurate information on a resume or application form. This could be more years of experience or higher educational level etc. The employer must take action within a reasonable time after discovering the mis-representation; otherwise, it is assumed that s/he has condoned the employee's performance.

4. Conflict of interest. For example: An employee's wife works for one of your company's suppliers so gives her company special deals.

5. Sabotage. You would have to be sure you could prove this.

6. Conviction of a criminal offence that:
   (a) Affects the attendance of employee.
   For example:
   If your employee is driving a company car and loses his/her licence to drive in some cases only, you can dismiss them. Employees who work in sales and who use their own vehicle and lose their licence to drive, can't be dismissed if they can provide a driver. An exception would be if it was a requirement of employment that they have a driver's licence.

   (b) Negates client's confidence in work done by employee.
   For example:
   An accountant charged with embezzlement looses client confidence, so the employer could dismiss the employee.

7. Fighting or threatening assaults. This can be on or off the business premises. Fighting or threats between workmates may or may not result in termination. Examine each case closely to see if there were extenuating circumstances.

8. Gross insubordination - refusal to do a task delegated by the supervisor (unless it is dangerous to themselves or others or is against safety or company regulations).

9. Serious breach of company rules.

10. Breach of safety rules.

11. Refusal to transfer. Whether or not an employee can be summarily dismissed for refusing to accept a transfer will depend on whether it is an express or implied term of his/her employment contract to take the transfer offered.

The employer must terminate the employee within a reasonable period of time after discovering the misconduct. The employer who knowingly accepts a certain standard of performance or misconduct may be said to have condoned such cause and may be prohibited from relying on such behaviour as grounds for dismissal.

Not immediate dismissal:

12. Intoxication (only after enough counselling from supervisor, attempts made to help employee obtain help from professionals and their condition has remained a chronic problem).
13. Illness - employee has chronic absences, had counselling and still is unable (because of absences) to fulfil the obligations of his/her position. Thankfully, most companies provide long-term disability to cover the more chronic diseases such as cancer, diabetes, multiple sclerosis, stroke, heart attack etc. This saves the manager the agony of having to let this type of employee go because of their absences.
14. Is unable, because of lack of ability to fulfil the obligations of his/her position. This inability is normally discovered during the employee's probationary period, but could crop up later at any time. Reasons could be that the employee is older and find they're unable to keep up with the normal flow and changes that occur in every job. Or it could be from such events as strokes, accidents or other disabilities.

I've only mentioned the situations that appear to give supervisors the most trouble.

How to investigate an incident:

1. Secure facts relating to misconduct.
2. Interview witnesses to obtain verifiable information
3. Obtain signed statements. Many observers are reluctant to 'get involved.' To accomplish this, take notes, verify the information with the witness and then ask them to initial or sign pages (preferable) that the information is correct. This is more effective than asking them to prepare a statement of what they witnessed. This will be easier for you to get the facts and employees are less likely to refuse to sign or initial the information.

4. Get all supporting documentation.
5. Get statistics and information regarding performance of other employees.
6. Hold meeting with employee to discuss the allegations of misconduct.
7. Make sure the employee has a chance to explain his/her actions.
8. Ensure that extenuating circumstances and explanations are fully explored and documented.
9. Analyse all facts obtained including those presented by the employee.
10. Determine if the facts (as presented) warrant that disciplinary action being taken. For example: Should the employee have been aware of the rule or regulation they broke?
11. If appropriate to the situation, determine corrective action required. Consider:
    - Previous record of the employee
    - Length of service
    - Whether or not the offence was an isolated incident on the employee's record
    - Was there provocation from others?
    - Was offence committed on the spur of the moment?
    - Was there evidence that employee was aware of rule/standard and that the rule/standards are being uniformly enforced with all employees?
    - Were there any extenuating factors?
    - Seriousness of the offence to the company
    - Other applicable factors
12. Inform employee of disciplinary decision.
13. Document the facts
14. Follow up with employee, including counselling on ways to prevent a re-occurrence.

A supervisor faces many disciplinary problems. It will help to keep in touch with other supervisors and managers - use their skill and knowledge to help you through the crisis. If you're lucky enough to have a Human Resources or Employee Relations branch of your company, ask them how you should deal with discipline problems preferably before they happen. If you're in a unionised company, know what's in your union agreements because it's up to you to enforce the rules in it. Ignorance is no longer a suitable excuse. Keep informed and up-to-date about content of company and employee manuals.

Exit Interviews:

These are meetings set up when an employee decides to leave your company voluntarily. Their input about problems they encountered can be a key to help you to keep your department running properly. Unfortunately, many employees worry about what kind of reference you'll give them, so play it safe and keep quiet about things you really need to know. This information may enable employers to cut down drastically on employee turnover especially if it is caused by a bad supervisor or manager.

If a pattern starts to appear in a department, higher management should ask themselves whether it may be because of the manager or department head in the area and ask pertinent questions of staff leaving the company.

When conducting exit interviews, it's important to ask open-ended questions. Let the employee know that you want to learn everything they have to say about the job they're leaving - both positive and negative. Ask them to be very honest with you so the company can overcome any reason they might have left that they perceive as being the company's fault.

Model exit interview:

(Company name) Exit Interview

Start by saying, *'Thank you for taking the time to speak with me regarding your resignation. (Company name) is committed to conducting exit interviews with all employees who make the decision to leave to obtain feedback and information that will ensure we create a working environment that encourages people to remain with (Company name) and to develop and grow within the business. All information obtained from this process will be held in the strictest of confidence.'*

Employee's Name:
Commenced:
Resignation Effective Date:

Department:
Position:
Supervisor:
Reason for resignation:
Purpose of exit interview:

1. Why are you leaving the company?
   - Working conditions
   - Better job offer
   - Relocation
   - Illness
   - Insufficient pay/benefits
   - Dislike work
   - Personality clash
   - Inconvenient working hours
   - Retirement
   - Workload
   - Location/transportation
   - Other. If other - please elaborate:
2. Can you give me an outline of the work you've been doing?
3. Is this the sort of work you expected to be doing when you joined (Company name)? Yes / No. If No, please explain:
4. Do you feel you received an adequate induction to (Company) the businesses policies and your duties and responsibilities? Yes / No. If no, what improvement could be made?
5. Do you feel the training for your position was adequate? Yes / No. If no, what improvements could be made?
6. Do you feel the level of responsibilities for your position was? Good _____ Not enough _____ Too much _____
7. Did you find your position was challenging? Yes / No. If not, why not?
8. How did you find the career and development opportunities available to you at (Company name)?
9. What did you enjoy most about working for (Company)?
10. What did you dislike most about working for (Company)?
11. Did you find your work colleagues pleasant, cooperative and good to work with? Yes / No. If No, please elaborate:
12. How well did you get along with your supervisor/manager?

13. To what degree was management supportive at (Company)? Was there an atmosphere of positive reinforcement and recognition? If no, what suggestions can you make to improve the situation?
14. Do you feel that (Company) has an environment that supports work/life balance? Yes / No If no, what suggestions can you make for improvement?
15. Do you feel the salary for your position is reasonable? Yes / No If not, why not?
16. Do you feel your pay increased sufficiently during your employment? Yes / No. If No, please explain:
17. Do you feel that (Company) benefits are reasonable? Yes / No. If no, why not? How could it be improved?
18. Would you recommend (Company name) as a place of employment to others? Yes / No. If no, why not?
19. If you are intending to go to another position, what does your new position offer you that (Company name) did not?
20. Do you have any further suggestions or comments you would like to offer?

Employee's signature:...
Date:...
Name of interviewer: ....
Position: ....
Where the interview held:......................................
Comments: ....
Signature of Interviewer ....
Date..

CONCLUSION

In the thirty-plus years I've been involved with Human Resources, I have learned that there are many ways of managing a Human Resources Department. However, if the person managing that department has not had the proper Human Resources training and are able to do the following – they and their company will flounder:

- Ensure that all employment laws are enforced
- Write Human Resources Policies and Procedures
- Prepare Employee Handbooks
- Hire the right employees to fill positions in the company
- Check references before employee is hired
- Write Job Descriptions
- Classify Positions
- Conduct Wage and Salary Surveys
- Do Manpower Planning
- Know how to train staff how to do Performance Appraisals
- Manage employee's confidential Personnel Files
- Find ways to keep employees motivated to do a good job
- Employee relations to deal with employee problems
- Liaise with management, union and employees
- Determine training needs
- Training and development of staff
- Manage training agreements
- Career development
- Conduct counselling interviews
- Conduct Disciplinary interviews
- Write written disciplinary warnings
- When necessary firing/terminating employees
- Laying off or making positions redundant when required

Please remember that the contents of this book are not to be construed as being professional advice. Readers must always check their Federal and State laws to ensure that they are acting according to their laws. Any decision made by the reader as a result of reading this book, is the sole responsibility of the reader.

HUMAN RESOURCES CONSULTING

Is your business too small to have someone on staff to deal exclusively with Human Resources matters?

If so, the following might interest you.

Cava Consulting offers the following Human Resource consulting services to companies too small to have their own Human Resources Department. After procedures are set up, one individual is trained to look after the H.R. function and thereafter we're on call to assist with further instructions.

ROBERTA CAVA has been in the Human Resources field for over thirty years. In 1982, she opened Cava Management Consulting Services in Canada, her second office in Maui, Hawaii in 1986, and then opened Cava Consulting on the Gold Coast of Australia in 1998 when she immigrated to Australia.

Her experience includes a position where she was Head of Human Resources, Payroll and Training for a financial firm in Melbourne and she set up and managed the Human Resources Department for a group of 12 construction companies based in Western Canada.

In addition to the above, Cava Consulting offers help in preparing company *Human Resources Policies and Procedures Manuals*

Our *Human Resources Policies and Procedures Manual* has over 300 pages of policies, procedures and forms used by Human Resource professionals.

The CD (*pdf)* locked version is **$395.00** (Aus$); and

The Word format (unlocked so you can adapt the information to meet your company's needs) - **$595.00**! (Having us custom-build these for companies can cost between $10,000 and $50,000 to prepare from scratch). We can still customise them for you and add your company logo at our hourly rate of **$150.00**.

We also:

- Prepare *Employee Handbooks*
- Identify what information should and should not be on employee personnel files
- Help you write job descriptions and classify positions for salary ranges (22,000 occupational profiles on disk)
- Teach supervisors how to document disciplinary matters and handle difficult matters such as female employees complaining of sexual harassment
- Set up a performance appraisal system that works! After set-up, your firm can implement and monitor it without assistance
- Conduct exit interviews (to determine reasons for high turnover of staff etc.)
- Recruit suitable staff
- Assess training needs
- Provide Career Counselling

Please contact Roberta Cava at:

info@dealingwithdifficultpeople.info

UNIQUE CAREER COUNSELLING SERVICE

Available via e-mail

Provided by ROBERTA CAVA of:

Cava Consulting,
105 / 3 Township Drive,
Burleigh Heads, Queensland.
4220, Australia.
Ph: 617 5535-0849

In these hard economic times, are you finding it difficult to find suitable employment in your field of work? How would you like to expand those opportunities? This unique career counselling service will enable you to determine your transferrable skills and identify another 20 to 40 occupations where you could use those skills.

An investment of **$175.00** (Aus) will provide you with an extensive report that includes:

- A list of your transferrable skills
- 20 to 30 primary and secondary occupations you could investigate that use your transferrable skills
- A psychological report that includes:

  1. Your strengths in the areas of interest, ability, values, personality, capacity
  2. Interest, ability and personality profiles
  3. What you think your skills are compared to what they really are
  4. Determine your management, persuasive, social artistic, clerical, mechanical, investigative and operational abilities
  5. Whether you are outgoing, reserved, factual, creative, analytical, caring organised or causal
  6. Your ability to think, reason and solve problems

7. Values inventory
8. Your stamina level
9. Your I.Q. Score
10. Performance and personality characteristics
11. Motivational and De-motivational factors
12. Whether you have what it takes to become an entrepreneur and have your own business

What will Happen?

After payment is made, you will be able to download a PowerPoint set of questions that you will complete. Some of the questions are timed and every question must be answered.

Your transferrable skills	10 questions
What do you like to do?	7
Timed Test (22 minutes):	30
Likes and Dislikes:	35
What kind of job do you prefer?	40
What kind of person are you?	11
How do you compare with others?	31
Describe your personality	23
Which do you prefer	15
Your preferences	8
Personality Profile	40
Total	**255 questions**

When you have completed the questions, you will e-mail the file to Roberta Cava. She will then do an analysis of your answers and e-mail you a detailed report (approximately 15 pages) including:

- Your interests and abilities
- Personality career reference results
- Capacity Score
- IQ Score
- Entrepreneurial profile results
- Values Inventory
- Job/Career Listings
- Samples of jobs based on applicant's tendencies

- o Primary
- o Secondary
- Personality Profile
  - o Personality in workplace
  - o Personality at home
- General characteristics
  - o Secondary characteristics
- Leadership method
- Decision-making method
- Stamina
- Performance Characteristics
- Personality Characteristics
- Motivational factors
- De-motivational factors

If you're interested in participating in this unique career counselling service, please go to our web page and follow the prompts:

www.dealingwithdifficultpeople.info/unique-career-counselling-service

For more information, contact Roberta Cava at:

rcava@dealingwithdifficultpeople.info

PERFORMANCE APPRAISAL SYSTEM

Roberta Cava is now selling her award-winning Performance Appraisal System that costs only $100.00 plus $1.00 (Aus$) per employee in your company. You can use the appraisal system thereafter for your employees. This is a very economical way for you to set up a Performance Appraisal system that works and is the best bargain you can buy.

Once you purchase the system you will be required to sign an agreement that the number of employees is correct and that you will only be using this system for your own employees. If you are a group of companies, each branch will need to purchase their own Performance Appraisal system.

Remember, performance appraisal systems that evaluate such subjective things as: judgement, initiative, attitude or interpersonal skills are *not* fair appraisal systems and should be replaced with performance appraisals that evaluate objective, measurable tasks.

Find out more by contacting: Roberta Cava at:

info@dealingwithdifficultpeople.info

BIBLIOGRAPHY

Betof, Edward; & Harwood, Frederic, *Just! How to survive and thrive in your first 12 months as a manager,* McGraw-Hill, 1992.

Cava, Roberta, *Dealing with Workplace Bullying – Society's Corporate Disgrace,* Cava Consulting, 2013.

Cava, Roberta, *Survival Skills for Supervisors and Managers,* Cava Consulting, 2013.

Effron, Marc, *Human resources in the 21st Century*, John Wiley & Sons, 2003.

Craig, R. L., *The ASTD Training and Development Handbook*; McGraw-Hill, 1996.

Grinckly, Richard, *Human Resources*, Barons Business Library Series, 2004

Hertzberg, F., Mauser, Bernard, & Snyderman, Barbara Bloch, *The Motivation to Work*, Transition Publishers, 1993.

Morgenstern, Julie o*rganizing from the Inside Out,* Owl Books, 1998.

Robbins,Stephen, *Supervision Today*, Prentice Hall, 2000.

Rosner, Bob, Halcrow, Allen & Levins, Alan S., *The Boss's Survival Guide*, McGraw-Hill, 2001

Ulrich, David, *Delivering Results; a New Mandate for HR Professionals*; Harvard Business School Press, 1998 and *Human Resources Champions, The Next agenda for adding value and delivering results*, Harvard Business School Press, 1997.

www.ingramcontent.com/pod-product-compliance
Lightning Source LLC
Chambersburg PA
CBHW071546200326
41519CB00021BB/6635